GCSE WJEC English
Reading Non-Fiction Texts
The Study Guide

This book is for anyone doing **GCSE WJEC English** or **GCSE WJEC English Language** at higher level.

It's a **step-by-step guide** to becoming an expert on the Unit 1: Reading: Non-Fiction Texts exam.

It's got **everything you need** — an exam-focused guide to analysing the texts, a sample exam and worked answers to help you get **the grade you want**.

It's ideal for use as a classroom study book or a revision guide.

What CGP is all about

Our sole aim here at CGP is to produce the highest quality books — carefully written, immaculately presented and dangerously close to being funny.

Then we work our socks off to get them out to you — at the cheapest possible prices.

CONTENTS

Section Four — Writing Techniques

Section Five — Exam Techniques

Section Six — The Exam

Section Seven — Sample Answers

Published by CGP

Editors:
Claire Boulter
Joe Brazier
Charley Darbishire
Edward Robinson
Caley Simpson
Jennifer Underwood

Produced With:
Emma Aubrey

Contributors:
Caroline Bagshaw
Lorraine Campbell
Graham Fletcher
Jane Harrison
Claire Hennighan
Nicola Woodfin

ISBN: 978 1 84762 108 5

With thanks to Heather Gregson, Kathryn Mawson and Julia Murphy for the proofreading.
With thanks to Laura Stoney for the copyright research.

The Publisher would like to thank the following copyright holders for permission to reproduce texts and images:

With thanks to iStockphoto.com for permission to reproduce the photographs used on pages 42 and 43.

Groovy website: www.cgpbooks.co.uk
Jolly bits of clipart from CorelDRAW®
Printed by Elanders Ltd, Newcastle upon Tyne.

Based on the classic CGP style created by Richard Parsons.

Non-Fiction Texts

This book will help you do better in your <u>Unit 1 exam</u> for <u>GCSE English</u> or <u>GCSE English Language</u>.*
This exam is on "Reading non-fiction texts".

The Assessment Objectives tell you what Skills you need

The <u>assessment objectives</u> are the things that WJEC says you need to be able to do to get <u>good marks</u> for this exam. Don't worry — there aren't very many of them. Put simply, you have to:

1) <u>Understand</u> what a text is <u>telling you</u> and use good <u>quotes</u> as <u>evidence</u> for your points. You'll also have to <u>compare</u> texts by looking for similarities and differences between them, and use appropriate <u>examples</u> to back up your points.

2) <u>Work out</u>, and show that you <u>understand</u>, what the writer's <u>ideas</u> are and what their <u>point of view</u> is.

3) Explain how writers use <u>language</u>, <u>grammar</u>, <u>layout</u> and <u>structure</u> to make their writing <u>effective</u>, and say how <u>effective</u> you think a text is in getting its <u>message</u> across to the <u>reader</u>.

Non-Fiction Texts are Pieces of Writing about Real Life

Non-fiction texts are about <u>real life</u> events, people and places, e.g.

fact sheets	information leaflets	biographies	autobiographies
travel writing		diaries	journals

Some texts are <u>written</u> specifically for the <u>media</u>. Media texts include <u>newspaper</u> articles, <u>magazine</u> articles, <u>advertisements</u> and <u>websites</u>. Media texts are generally <u>non-fiction</u> — e.g. newspaper articles about real-life issues.

'Media' is any way of communicating with large numbers of people, e.g. newspapers and TV.

Although non-fiction texts are based on real life, they often contain the <u>personal opinions</u> of the writer. They might only give you <u>one version of events</u>. Don't expect a piece of writing to be balanced, dry and academic just because it's non-fiction...

This book doubles up as a rather fetching hat...

This book is full of straightforward ways of getting <u>extra marks</u> in the Unit 1 exam on reading non-fiction texts. The best way to use the book is to read through the explanations and examples and practise all the tips. Then try to include as many as you can in your work.

you're in Wales, your exam might be structured differently, but this book will still be useful. Ask your teacher for more information.

The Audience

When you're reading a non-fiction text, you've got to think about the audience — the people that the writer wants to read their work.

Writers aim their work at a Specific Audience

The writer will always have a specific group of people in mind as their audience when they write.

e.g.

TEXT	AUDIENCE
Article in 'The Financial Times'	Business people
Travel guide book	Holiday-makers
Problem page in 'Sugar'	Teenage girls

Some texts will have more than one audience, e.g. toy adverts will try to appeal to the kids who use them but also to the parents who have to buy them.

Content and Form can show who the audience is

1) Sometimes you can work out who the audience is by the text's content (subject matter), e.g. an article in 'Top Gear' magazine about cars is obviously aimed at someone who's into cars.

2) The form (the way a text is laid out) can also tell you who the intended audience is. E.g. a large font and lots of pictures means it's probably for children, but if there's lots of text crammed into dense columns, it's more likely to be intended for adults.

Betty often bought "Top Gear" for herself, and "Medieval Role Play" for Bert.

Language can give you plenty of clues too

1) The vocabulary (choice of words) can tell you about the target audience, e.g. about the age group

> Today, we witnessed a discussion on fox-hunting. As one can imagine, this issue, although it has been debated for many years, still managed to elicit mixed emotions from all concerned.

Difficult vocabulary, e.g. saying 'elicit' rather than just 'bring out', and complex sentences show this text is aimed at adults.

> Dungeon Killer 3 is the hottest new game of the year! There are 52 amazing levels and 6 cool new characters — don't miss out on the wildest gaming experience of your life!

Modern slang and simple sentences show this is aimed at younger people.

2) The language can also give you clues about the target audience's level of understanding:

> The object of a game of football is to get the ball in the opposing team's goal. Sounds easy, doesn't it? Well, firstly, the other team has the same thing in mind. Secondly, there are eleven of them who are trying to stop you.

Simple, general explanations show this is for beginners.

> The next hole was a par-3 and I hit my tee shot directly onto the green. Sadly my putting let me down badly and I ended up getting a bogey.

Technical vocabulary shows this is for people who know a bit about the sport.

Hello? Is there anybody there?

You need to work out who the intended audience is so that you can discuss the writer's intentions, techniques, and how successful they are. Keep the audience in mind throughout your answer.

The Purpose of the Text

Another big thing you need to work out about the text you get in the exam is: "What is the writer's <u>purpose</u>?" In other words, "<u>Why</u> has the writer written this?" Why indeed.

There are some <u>Common Purposes</u> <u>of writing</u>

The <u>purpose</u> of the text means the <u>reason</u> that it has been written — what the writer is <u>trying to do</u>. Non-fiction texts are often written for <u>one or more</u> of these reasons:

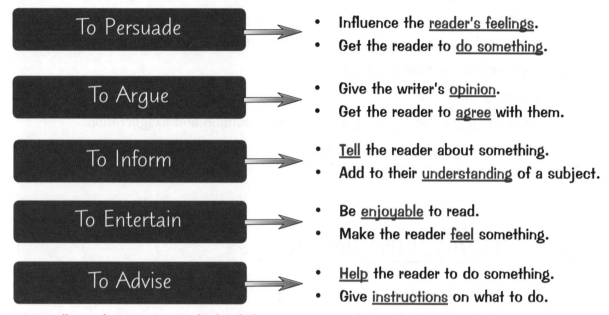

To Persuade
- Influence the <u>reader's feelings</u>.
- Get the reader to <u>do something</u>.

To Argue
- Give the writer's <u>opinion</u>.
- Get the reader to <u>agree</u> with them.

To Inform
- <u>Tell</u> the reader about something.
- Add to their <u>understanding</u> of a subject.

To Entertain
- Be <u>enjoyable</u> to read.
- Make the reader <u>feel</u> something.

To Advise
- <u>Help</u> the reader to do something.
- Give <u>instructions</u> on what to do.

Pages 4-8 tell you how to spot which of these purposes the writer has in mind, and how you can <u>discuss</u> them in the exam.

<u>Tone</u> <u>and</u> <u>Style</u> <u>are closely related</u>

1) In the same way that there are different <u>tones of voice</u> when people speak, e.g. calm, angry, friendly, there are different <u>tones</u> that writers can use.

2) <u>Style</u> is to do with the type of language and techniques a writer uses, for example formal or informal.

3) Writers choose a style and tone that's appropriate for the <u>audience</u> they're writing for and the <u>purpose</u> of the writing.

> There's more about tone and style on p.9-10.

When you're reading a non-fiction text, remember to think about:
- <u>who</u> the author is writing for (audience)
- what they're <u>trying to do</u> (purpose)
- <u>how</u> they write (style and tone)
- to what extent you think they <u>succeed</u>.

WARNING: Being too informal can lead to dire consequences.

My life has no purpose — but I do have a dog that barks...

Some texts have more than one purpose, e.g. travel books are often meant to entertain, as they're full of interesting stories, but they're usually informative too, telling you about great places to go.

Texts that Persuade

Some texts have the purpose of <u>persuading</u> you to do something, like donate money to save a rare species of hamster, or something like that anyway.

Persuasive Writing tries to get you to Do Something

1) <u>Persuasive</u> writing tries to get the reader to do something, e.g. to support a charity, buy a product or try a new activity.

2) Persuasive writing often uses these <u>techniques</u> to <u>influence the reader</u>:

   • using <u>light-hearted, friendly language</u> that creates a bond with the reader

   • appealing to the reader's <u>emotions</u>

   • <u>flattering</u> the reader

   • using <u>rhetorical techniques</u> (see p.17) like repetition and exaggeration.

3) <u>Media texts</u> are often <u>persuasive</u>, e.g. an <u>advertisement</u> persuading you to buy a new game or a travel <u>website</u> persuading you that Slough is a great place for a holiday.

Persuasive writing looks like this

Uses exaggeration to make the film seem important. →

Question appeals directly to the reader. →

> The Tarnished is the best British film since Get Carter. It buzzes with fresh ideas, sharp dialogue and inspired acting. Catch it while you can — you'll feel a fool if you miss it.
> The Tarnished will be showing at art-house cinemas next week, before a multiplex release later in the month. Surely, this is the 'Great British Film' we have all been waiting for?

← Tells the reader what to do.

← Uses "we" to create a bond with the reader.

Write about texts that persuade Like This

Back up your points with quotes. →

> The writer uses rhetorical techniques to make the writing more persuasive. For example, the writer uses exaggeration, describing the movie as "the best British film since Get Carter". The confidence and optimism of this statement helps to persuade the reader that the film is exciting and unmissable.

← Show that you understand the effect of the writer's techniques.

Persuasive texts are great, don't you agree? Yes you do...

There's often a persuasive text in the Unit 1 exam so it's really important to understand the writing techniques used and the effect these have on the reader. There's more information about these techniques in the next few sections. Keep on reading, folks...

Texts that Argue

Another common purpose of texts is to <u>argue</u> a point, to get the reader to agree with it.

Writing to Argue is all about Opinions

1) When people write to <u>argue</u>, they want to make the reader <u>agree with their opinion</u>.

2) They try to write <u>clearly</u> and <u>forcibly</u> to get their points across, e.g. in newspaper editorials.

3) Writing to argue <u>isn't the same</u> as having an argument with somebody. Writers will usually be <u>polite</u> when they're arguing a point — they want to get the reader <u>on their side</u>.

4) Writing to argue is <u>quite similar</u> to writing to <u>persuade</u> — but writers tend to focus on changing the <u>reader's opinion</u>, rather than encouraging them to take action.

5) Writers use plenty of techniques to make their arguments <u>more effective</u>, e.g.

- <u>backing up</u> their argument with facts and statistics
- using <u>quotes from experts</u> who agree with their argument
- explaining why <u>other points of view</u> are wrong
- using <u>rhetorical techniques</u> (see p.17) like repetition and rhetorical questions.

Writing to Argue looks like this

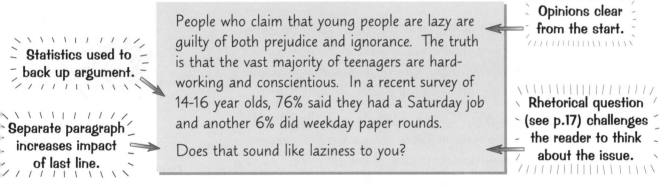

Statistics used to back up argument.

Separate paragraph increases impact of last line.

People who claim that young people are lazy are guilty of both prejudice and ignorance. The truth is that the vast majority of teenagers are hard-working and conscientious. In a recent survey of 14-16 year olds, 76% said they had a Saturday job and another 6% did weekday paper rounds.

Does that sound like laziness to you?

Opinions clear from the start.

Rhetorical question (see p.17) challenges the reader to think about the issue.

Write about texts that argue Like This

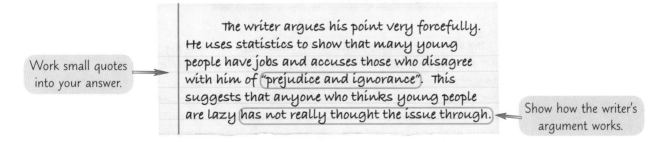

Work small quotes into your answer.

The writer argues his point very forcefully. He uses statistics to show that many young people have jobs and accuses those who disagree with him of "prejudice and ignorance". This suggests that anyone who thinks young people are lazy has not really thought the issue through.

Show how the writer's argument works.

I h8 U — I h8 U 2...

If a writer is trying to argue a point, it's all about getting the reader to see things from their point of view. It won't be balanced, like a discussion — it'll be one-sided, with evidence that's carefully chosen because it supports their point of view.

Texts that Inform

If the purpose of a text is to <u>inform</u> you, the writer's aim is to pass on knowledge to you as clearly and effectively as possible. Informative texts have lots of <u>facts</u> and usually a <u>straightforward style</u>.

Informative Writing Tells You *something*

1) Informative texts give the reader <u>facts and information</u>. This could be:

- <u>what has happened</u> — e.g. a bank statement or a history book
- <u>what will or might happen</u> — e.g. a weather forecast
- <u>something you might need to know</u> — e.g. a **TV** guide or travel guide
- <u>to advertise something</u> — e.g. a magazine advert or a brochure

2) Informative writing can be used simply to help the reader <u>understand</u> something, as in a school textbook.

3) But information can be sneakily used to give an <u>opinion</u> on something — e.g. a newspaper may <u>carefully pick</u> information that supports a particular political party. Even though a newspaper article may not say outright what its opinion is, it can still be <u>biased</u>.

Bias is when the writer's own opinions affect their writing, so that it leans towards a particular opinion — see page 18.

Informative Writing *looks like this*

Gives you specific details and dates.

The Mini first went on sale in 1959. It soon became the best selling car in Europe. Over five million of them were made and many famous people including the Beatles bought them.

The Mini Cooper S version won the Monte Carlo Rally in 1964. Minis were less expensive than many other cars. Now they are made by BMW and aimed at a different market.

There were moments when Hank regretted buying a cheap and affordable car.

Contains facts rather than opinions.

Write *about informative texts* Like This

Make a clear opening point.

Use quotes to back up your points.

The author gives a positive impression of the Mini by giving a lot of details about its history. The fact that "Over five million of them were made" gives an impression of how successful they were. This is reinforced when the author informs us that "famous people including the Beatles bought them". This fact adds to the sense that the cars were popular and fashionable.

Build on your ideas.

Explain the effect of the quote.

If there are lots of facts and figures, it's informative...

You need to show you can recognise informative writing and explain how it's used. Don't assume it's obvious — spell out to the examiner exactly what the writer is informing us about, why they're doing it and how effective you think they are. Make sure you point out if the information is biased.

Texts that Entertain

Entertaining texts are ones that you would read for <u>pleasure</u>. There are less of the cold, hard (and sometimes a teeny bit dull) facts of informative writing and more of the kind of things that make you <u>scared</u>, <u>excited</u> or <u>amused</u>. That's more of the fun stuff, then...

Entertaining Writing aims to be Enjoyable to read

1) Entertaining writing is meant to be <u>interesting</u>. People read it mostly for <u>fun</u> (although they might <u>learn</u> something at the same time). Travel books are a good example of entertaining non-fiction writing.

2) The author might entertain the reader with <u>anecdotes</u> (stories of <u>funny things</u> that happened to them). Or they might use <u>entertaining descriptions and comparisons</u> of things or people.

3) Entertaining writing has more <u>creative</u> and <u>unexpected</u> bits than informative writing.

Entertaining Writing looks like this

This piece of writing is on the same subject as the one on page 6 — but this one is <u>entertaining</u>. Have a look at how it's different from the informative one.

Interesting similes and comparisons.

> My first car was a 1970 Mini. I loved it from the moment I sat in it. It went like a rocket. By that I mean it always had smoke coming out of its rear end! Perhaps I shouldn't have tried to drive it like Michael Caine.
>
> It was a subtle shade of bright orange and should have come complete with free executive sunglasses. Still, I was a student then and they wouldn't have fitted my image.

Contains funny images.

Tells a story.

Write about entertaining texts Like This

Make an opening point.

> The author gains the reader's attention by using the first person ("I") in her writing. That makes her experiences seem more real. She uses humour to maintain interest. For example "It always had smoke coming out of its rear end!" paints an entertaining picture and the exclamation mark reinforces the effect of the joke. The comical contrast of "subtle shade" and "bright orange" helped me to visualise the car and enjoy the description.

Use evidence from the text.

Give a personal reaction — this shows you're enthusiastic about it.

Nobby found the new Bill Bryson book most entertaining.

Writing exam answers — now that's entertainment...

Some texts will be both informative and entertaining, e.g. a travel book may contain useful facts about a place but also give you some funny anecdotes about what happened when the author was there. Try to work out which bits of the text inform and which entertain when you write about them.

Texts that Advise

When people write to advise, they're trying to help the reader to <u>do something</u>, or to make the right <u>decision</u>. The style is clearer and less emotional than writing that argues or persuades.

Writing to Advise sounds Clear and Calm

1) When people are writing to advise, they want their readers to <u>follow their suggestions</u>.

2) The tone is <u>calm</u> and <u>less emotional</u> than writing that argues or persuades.

3) The advice is usually <u>clearly written and laid out</u>. The writer may use bullet points or numbered lists to make it easier to follow.

4) The style may be <u>formal</u>, e.g. in a letter from your bank offering financial advice, or <u>informal</u>, e.g. in a magazine advice column (see pages 9-10).

> <u>Instructive texts</u> are texts that give you advice on something very specific in a step-by-step way — like assembly instructions for furniture.

"Congratulations on purchasing your new TS-522-A shell..."

Writing to Advise looks like this

Addresses the reader using the second person ("you").

> Before you buy a pension, you need to be sure that it is the right one for you — dropping out can mean that you lose a lot of the money you've already paid in. You should look at the pension company's reputation, past results and penalties for changing schemes.

Friendly warning.

Uses specific details to give practical advice.

Write about texts that advise Like This

Remember to explain the effect of the quote.

These paragraphs both use P.E.E.D. (Point, Example, Explain, Develop). See page 33 for more on this.

Show that you know what effect it will have on the reader.

> The writer uses a friendly, no-nonsense tone to get her advice across in a clear, accessible way. When she says, "you need to be sure", it sounds as if she is talking to a friend. This makes the reader more likely to take the advice, as it seems well-meant and helpful.
>
> The language that the writer uses is specific but uncomplicated. She gives detailed advice, such as "look at the pension company's reputation, past results and penalties". This makes the writer seem well-informed and knowledgeable. As a result, the reader is more likely to think that the advice is worthwhile, and act on it.

Develop the point — say why the writer has chosen this style.

Talk about the writer's use of language.

Explain what sort of impression this type of language creates.

Texts that advise are clearly presented and easy to follow

Texts that advise generally assume you're already on the writer's side — people usually choose to read them because they want to know about something and they trust the writer's opinion. Because of this, they usually sound more friendly and less "in-your-face" than texts that argue or persuade.

Formal Writing

Formal writing sounds polite or "correct" — the sort of writing you'd use in coursework. It tends to use an impersonal tone — the writer doesn't try to be matey.

There are a few ways of Spotting Formal Writing

1) It's quite easy to recognise a formal style of writing. Just think about the way a letter from your teacher or a newspaper article would be written.

2) Here are a few common features of formal writing:

> - a dry or "stuffy" tone (not exciting or emotional)
> - standard English — no slang or abbreviations
> - long, complex sentences with correct punctuation
> - sounds impersonal — the writer doesn't try to relate to you
> - written in the third person — "he", "she", "they" etc.
> - you don't get a sense of the writer's personality
> - no jokes or light-hearted comments

When the writer mentioned 'pâté' for the third time, Jeremy felt it related to him just a little too much.

3) Pieces of writing that are usually written in a formal style include:

- textbooks
- charity appeals
- business letters
- instruction manuals
- news reports
- job adverts

Formal Writing looks like this

Long sentence. →

Avoids shortened words — "it is" instead of "it's".

> When wiring an electrical plug it is always necessary to follow the safety instructions in order to avoid personal injury or death. It is easy to suffer serious harm and ignoring the instructions is simply not worth the risk. Some people believe that it is better to leave this kind of work to qualified electricians.

← Sounds strict.

Opinion is given in an impersonal tone.

Write about formal writing Like This

Say what style the writer uses.

Give an example.

> The writer creates a formal style by using long sentences and avoiding talking directly to the reader. For example, he says "it is always necessary to" instead of "you have to". The formal style helps to add to the impact of the information. I think it is effective because it gives an impression of how dangerous it would be if you did not follow the advice.

Show how the formal style works.

Say if you think it works and why.

One is undoubtedly required to discuss formal writing...

Basically, if a text sounds like it's been written by a teacher or a bank manager, it's formal. As usual, you need to say why the writer has chosen to use this style and tone — think about who they're writing for and what message they're trying to give, and say how the formal style helps them do this.

Informal Writing

Informal writing sounds as if someone is <u>chatting</u> to you. It sounds more friendly and casual than formal writing. Writers use a <u>personal tone</u> to try to build up a relationship with the reader.

Informal Writing *sounds chatty*

1) If writing is clearly <u>not formal</u>, it's — wait for it — <u>informal</u>. Tricky eh?

2) Here are a few common <u>features</u> of informal writing:

> - a chatty, personal tone — as if the writer is talking to you
> - written in the first person — "I", "me", "my", "our", "we" etc.
> - has a sense of the author's personality, opinions and emotions
> - non-standard English — e.g. abbreviations and slang
> - short, simple sentences
> - jokes and a light-hearted tone

Light-hearted Tone was a perfect match for Carefree Meg.

3) Pieces of writing that are often written in an <u>informal style</u> include:

- teenage magazine articles
- adverts aimed at young people
- gossip columns
- travel writing

Informal Writing *looks like this*

Personal opinion.

Use of humour emphasises personal voice.

> School uniform should be banned. As if it isn't bad enough wearing a manky, itchy jumper most of the time, the PE kit we have to wear was designed for the 1950s. Mine was bought in Year 7 and it's ridiculously tight now. Then in Science, the lab coat and safety goggles make me look like a short-sighted lollipop lady.

Written in first person.

Write *about informal writing Like This*

Say what effect the personal style has.

> The informal style allows the writer to express her views very directly and forcefully. By writing in the first person, she seems to be speaking directly to the reader. She says her science clothes "make me look like a short-sighted lollipop lady". This humorous image highlights how silly the uniform is.
>
> Her personal tone is also effective in showing how much she hates her "manky, itchy jumper". This description emphasises how uncomfortable she feels, and many pupils will be able to empathise with her.

Use the correct technical terms.

Explain why the quote is effective.

Work short quotes into your sentences.

Informal writing helps the reader relate to the writer...

The formality or informality of a piece of writing is all about the way it's expressed, rather than what it actually says. Remember to explain who the writing is aimed at, what the writer is trying to do, how the writer is trying to do it, and how well you think the writer has done it.

Features of an Argument

If you're going to talk about a writer's argument in your answer, the first thing you need to do is <u>follow</u> the argument — in other words, <u>understand what points they're making</u>.

Look out for the Main Features of an Argument

A writer can use lots of different <u>techniques</u> when they argue a point. These might include:

- <u>facts</u> — see page 13.
- <u>opinions</u> — either the author's or someone else's. See page 14.
- <u>implications</u> — where the writer suggests something is the case without saying it outright, e.g. "Ever since Kelvin moved in, things have started mysteriously disappearing."
- <u>generalisations</u>, <u>counter-arguments</u>, <u>rhetoric</u> and <u>bias</u> — see pages 15-18.

All of these can be used either very obviously and deliberately, or more subtly. When you're following an argument, you have to spot <u>when</u> one of these turns up in the text, and say what <u>effect</u> it has.

Identify the Key Points of the argument

To follow an argument, you need to identify the <u>key points</u> — the main reasons the writer gives to back up their argument.

You can often spot where one key point ends and another one begins by the writer's use of <u>paragraphs</u>. A new paragraph often means a new key point:

In this increasingly stressful age it is important that young people find the time to relax and enjoy the best years of their life. With exam after exam, modern teenagers hardly have time to take a break and have fun with their friends.

> The key point of the first paragraph is that schoolwork can prevent teenagers from enjoying themselves.

On top of the gruelling demands from school, the attitudes of well-meaning but demanding parents often do not help. The constant query of "Have you done your biology revision yet?" can only add to the stress and frustration of having to give up the opportunity of fun for more schoolwork.

> The second paragraph moves onto a related but different point — the problems caused by parents.

Another way of spotting where a new point starts is when you see <u>linking words and phrases</u>:

| however | secondly | furthermore | on the other hand | in addition |

Taxi! Follow that argument...

If you try to talk about the whole text in one go, you'll more than likely end up in a sticky mess on the floor. But if you break an argument down into its main points, you'll find it a lot easier to discuss how the writer makes their points and how effective they are — see next page...

Evaluating an Argument

Evaluating an argument means saying how <u>effective</u> it is. You need to say whether or not you think it will successfully persuade the reader to agree with the writer, and why.

Say What's Good about the argument

1) It's <u>not enough</u> just to say an argument is good. You need to say <u>how</u> the writer makes their points and <u>why</u> they're effective.

2) Think about what kind of <u>impression</u> (e.g. forceful, emotional, knowledgeable) the writer creates with the language they use, and <u>how</u> this impression helps to <u>persuade</u> the reader.

Unfortunately this isn't the key to a good answer.

Evaluate an argument Like This

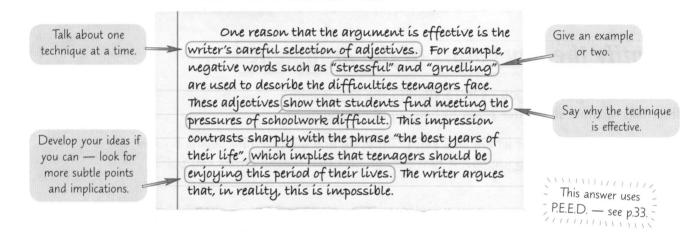

Talk about one technique at a time.

Develop your ideas if you can — look for more subtle points and implications.

> One reason that the argument is effective is the writer's careful selection of adjectives. For example, negative words such as "stressful" and "gruelling" are used to describe the difficulties teenagers face. These adjectives show that students find meeting the pressures of schoolwork difficult. This impression contrasts sharply with the phrase "the best years of their life", which implies that teenagers should be enjoying this period of their lives. The writer argues that, in reality, this is impossible.

Give an example or two.

Say why the technique is effective.

This answer uses P.E.E.D. — see p.33.

The argument might have some Drawbacks

You might think some parts of an argument aren't convincing, and if that's what you reckon, <u>say so</u>. But if you do say this, make sure you've got some darn good <u>reasons</u> for saying so — if you just say, "the writer's argument is really stupid, he's missed the point", you won't get good marks.

> Here are some criticisms you might be able to make:
>
> 1) <u>Inconsistencies</u> — sometimes a writer says things that contradict each other.
>
> 2) <u>Inaccuracies</u> — the writer's information might just be plain <u>wrong</u>. Watch out though — you have to really know your stuff before you go saying a point is inaccurate.
>
> 3) <u>Dullness</u> — sometimes an argument just won't grab you. This might be because it's <u>full of statistics</u> and not much else, or because the text is <u>confusing</u> or <u>unclear</u>. As always, if you can give examples of this, you'll pick up marks.

It was terrible! It wasn't that bad! It was great! MORE!

In your exam, you might be given a text that's presenting an argument. You need to be able to analyse the text by evaluating the argument and saying how successful it is. It's usually easiest to say mostly positive things, but try to include one or two criticisms too, to make your answer balanced.

Facts

In your exam, it'll be useful if you can <u>spot facts and opinions</u> in texts and say what <u>effect</u> they have. Best get your head around the <u>difference</u> between them then...

Facts <u>are definitely</u> True...

FACT: Manchester United won the UEFA Champions League in May 2008.

FACT: Two metres of string is longer than one metre of string.

FACT: Barack Obama was the President of the United States after George W. Bush.

y degree in accountancy really helped
e further my career at Oceanworld.

...apart from *False Facts* — they're *Untrue*

False facts are things that can be <u>proved</u> to be <u>untrue</u>, like these:

FALSE FACT: My nose is fifteen centimetres long.

FALSE FACT: Madonna's real name is Derek Tyson.

Write about Facts *like this...*

Make your point.

The author uses facts in the text to strengthen his argument that Carl Lewis is the greatest sprinter and long jumper in history. For example, he mentions Lewis's nine Olympic gold medals, two world records for the 100 metres, and 65 consecutive long jump competition victories. Each fact is evidence of Lewis' great success, adding weight to the author's case. However, I think the author's argument could be improved by comparing Carl Lewis to other successful sprinters and long-jumpers.

You could use "for example" to start your examples — it makes it dead clear to the examiner what you're doing.

Explain why the author has used facts.

Develop your point.

Not *like this...*

Any fool can count the facts and say where they are. It's a <u>classic mistake</u>. Don't do it.

This answer is poor because it doesn't say how the facts help the writer's argument.

The author uses four facts in this text. There are two on line 2 and another two on line 5. He thinks that Carl Lewis is the greatest sprinter and long-jumper in the history of athletics.

Quote the facts — don't just say where they are like this answer does.

> 1 < > 2 <

"Line 1 is longer than line 2" — fact, false fact or opinion...?

FACT — gorillas are hairier than slugs...

...except bald gorillas of course. Anyway, make sure you can spot the facts in a piece of text, and say how the author uses them to get their point across. Then go and shave a gorilla.

Opinions

Now you know a bit about facts, it's time for <u>opinions</u>.

Opinions aren't True or Untrue — they're just Beliefs

Different people can see the same thing in <u>different ways</u>. These are opinions, not facts — they're just what someone <u>thinks</u>. You <u>can't prove</u> that an opinion is true or untrue.

> The words "I think" show that this is just a point of view.

OPINION:	I think that animal testing for cosmetics should be banned.
OPINION:	CD singles won't exist in ten years' time.

> You can't prove this one way or the other yet.

Opinions can be given as <u>direct speech</u> (as if it's <u>spoken</u> by the <u>writer</u>), like in the two examples abo
They can also be given as <u>reported dialogue</u> (spoken by <u>someone else</u>). This can make the opinions
much more <u>convincing</u>.

EXAMPLE:	A leading scientist says that animal testing for cosmetics should be banned.

> This opinion is more convincing because it's what an expert thinks.

Some sentences contain both Opinions AND Facts

Sometimes you can get opinions and facts in the <u>same sentence</u>. Like this one:

FACT AND OPINION:	Manchester United gloriously won the UEFA Champions League in May 2008.

> The word "gloriously" is just an opinion...

> ...but the second bit is fact.

This kind of writing is often a <u>sign of bias</u>. Read more about bias on page 18.

Write about Opinions like this...

> Mention all the effects the opinions have.

The many opinions in this text reinforce the author's points and
give the text an informal tone. The author uses satirical opinions to mock
the target of her argument. For example: "Jamie Smith comes second in
the contest for the World's most irritating display of chirpiness only to
my three year old nephew at four o'clock on Christmas morning." The
strength and humour of these opinions create a powerful image in the
reader's mind, making the author's argument more persuasive. The
light-hearted tone suggests that the author's intention is to make fun
of Jamie Smith, rather than to seriously criticise him.

> Explain why the author has used opinions.

> Develop your point — e.g. comment on how the opinions reveal the author's attitude.

In my opinion, Hugh Jackman is extremely good-looking...

If a text presents different opinions, you might need to compare them. There are certain phrases
that will help you to do this. Here's a few: similar to, contrasting with, on the other hand, different
from, however, in agreement with, unlike, in the same way, conversely. All very useful.

Generalisations

Generalisations are sweeping statements that aren't necessarily true, like "young people today have no respect", or "Reality TV stars are all dim-witted, money-grabbing losers".

Generalisations make an argument more Forceful

1) A generalisation is a statement that's presented confidently as fact but doesn't give details.
2) Generalisations often make an argument sound more forceful and convincing when it's actually not all that accurate.
3) They can be misleading — they often conveniently ignore facts that don't support them.
4) Generalisations sometimes create unfair stereotypes — e.g. "Foreign footballers are all cheats."

Generalisations look like this

Chips are bad for you.

Although it's true that eating loads of chips is unhealthy, most people reckon they're OK every now and again. Also, some types of chips are worse than others.

Smokers trying to quit usually have more success if they use nicotine patches.

The statement gives no proof to back up this claim, but it sounds convincing.

Generalisations like this are often used in adverts, to try to give a positive impression of the product.

Write about generalisations Like This

In the exam, it'll be helpful if you can identify any generalisations and write about what effect they have.

Here's your point, made right at the start of your paragraph.

Here is your example.

Here's your explanation.

The advertisement uses a generalisation when it says that "Smokers trying to quit usually have more success if they use nicotine patches." This is presented as a fact in order to convince the audience to buy the patches. However, I don't think it's a very effective advertisement, because no scientific evidence is given to back up the generalisation that's been used.

This is where you develop your point.

Generalisation — an army promotion?

People use generalisations all the time. They're often used to exaggerate the truth, or to present a one-sided version of it, with carefully selected evidence that doesn't give the full story. If you can spot where a writer's used one, you can argue that their argument isn't as strong as it might seem.

Counter-arguments

Writers will often quote the <u>opposite point of view</u> first, then <u>argue against it</u>. This is a counter-argument — it strengthens the writer's own opinion by making it seem more reasonable.

Counter-arguments Disagree with the original argument

1) A counter-argument is when a writer presents one point of view, then <u>disagrees</u> with it, showing <u>why</u> it's <u>wrong</u>.

2) This makes the <u>writer's opinion</u> seem <u>better</u> in comparison.

3) Using a counter-argument shows that the writer has <u>considered other viewpoints</u>, instead of just jumping to an opinion. It makes them seem like a sensible, <u>thoughtful</u> person, instead of some ranting nutter.

Counter-arguments look like this

> Although many parents believe that eight hours' sleep is needed to learn effectively at school, studies show that the necessary amount actually varies greatly between different teenagers.

The first bit states an argument.

The second bit is the counter-argument — it picks holes in the original argument.

Write about counter-arguments Like This

First point out how the <u>original argument</u> and the <u>counter-argument</u> are made.

Show what the writer's counter-argument is.

The writer presents the argument from the adult point of view when she says, "many parents believe that eight hours' sleep is needed to learn effectively", but then goes on to counter this argument by claiming that "the necessary amount actually varies greatly between different teenagers."

Show how the writer describes the original argument.

Then say <u>how</u> this technique strengthens the writer's argument — look at the <u>language</u> used.

Use quotes to show how the two sides of the argument come across differently.

The word "believe" makes the parents' point of view sound unconvincing, as if there is no basis for it. The mention of "studies", on the other hand, makes the writer's own opinion sound well-informed. This makes the writer's point of view sound stronger and more valid than that of the parents.

Describe the effect of presenting the arguments in this way

It doesn't mean disagreements between tables then...

Writers often present the opposite point of view as uninformed and irrational. They can then show their own opinion to be more sensible and well-researched. Another thing they can do is take specific things about the opposing point of view and one by one show that they're false.

Rhetoric

Rhetoric is when writers use <u>techniques</u> to make language more <u>persuasive</u> and <u>convincing</u>. The idea is to persuade their audience that there is only one sensible viewpoint — theirs.

Rhetorical Questions *don't need an answer*

1) Rhetorical questions are phrased to make the answer seem so <u>obvious</u> it's not even worth saying.
2) This makes the reader feel like they're <u>making their own mind up</u>, when actually the writer is deliberately trying to get them to think a <u>certain way</u>.

e.g. Can it really be fair to set students these ridiculous and unnecessary assignments?

The words "ridiculous" and "unnecessary" are put there to get the reader to think, "No, of course it's not fair."

Repetition *emphasises key points*

1) Writers <u>repeat</u> words or phrases to <u>emphasise</u> their most important points.
2) They're often repeated in <u>threes</u> (this is called the <u>rule-of-three</u>).

e.g. It's outrageous to suggest that pupils don't work hard. It's outrageous to suggest that we should give up all our free time for study. Most of all though, it's outrageous to expect us to take on even more homework.

Write *about rhetoric* Like This

As always, make a <u>point</u>, give an <u>example</u>, explain the <u>effect</u> and <u>develop</u> your point.

Say what effect the repeated word has — don't assume it's obvious.

The writer uses many rhetorical devices to persuade the reader that students should not be given more homework to do. For example, his repetition of the word "outrageous" shows us how angry he feels about the idea. It also allows him to link together his different points, to show there are many reasons why he disagrees with those in favour of more homework.

This is a just a clever way of saying "types of rhetoric".

Develop your point about the effect of the rhetoric to get top marks.

Exams are great, exams are great, exams are great...

There are lots of other <u>rhetorical techniques</u>, for example using emotive language (see page 29) or exaggerated language (see page 18) to add to the text's impact.

Bias

If a text is biased, it <u>doesn't</u> give a <u>balanced</u> view. The writer's own point of view affects the writing, so it gives a misleading impression of the facts.

Biased Writing *is affected by the writer's opinions*

1) Biased writers don't usually lie, but they <u>don't give the full picture</u>.

2) Sometimes the writer <u>won't mention</u> something that opposes their argument, or they'll <u>exaggerate</u> something that supports it. Exaggerated language, e.g. 'Wayne Rooney is the greatest striker in the history of football', is also known as <u>hyperbole</u> (pronounced hi-PER-bow-lee).

3) Bias <u>isn't always obvious</u>, or even deliberate. Biased writers don't always make their opinion clear. They often <u>seem</u> to be talking in a neutral, factual way — while actually only presenting one point of view.

4) You need to be able to <u>recognise</u> bias, so that you don't mistake opinion for fact.

5) Biased writing often uses <u>generalisations</u> (see page 15).

Bias *looks like this*

> Coldplay are simply the best band to come out of this country since the Beatles. They have produced hit after hit on a regular basis, and perform to huge sell-out crowds. Their music is distinctive and yet subtle — it grabs you immediately and yet continues to offer new levels of creativity with every subsequent listen.

Jim Dodd and the Budgies
— stiff competition.

1) The text above <u>ignores</u> the fact that lots of other bands have lots of hits and play to big audiences.

2) There's <u>no hard evidence</u> there — no facts and figures to back up the writer's claims.

3) The last sentence is just <u>opinion</u> — lots of people might completely <u>disagree</u> with this.

Write *about bias Like This*

Make a clear opening point.

Say if you think there's something missing from the writer's argument.

The writer is clearly biased in favour of Coldplay. He mentions "hit after hit" and "huge sell-out crowds", but does not give any details. There is no criticism and there are no comparisons with other bands to support the claim that they are the best "since the Beatles". This clear bias detracts from the writer's argument as he appears to have jumped to his opinion without finding any proper evidence for it.

Support it with short quotes.

Say what the overall effect of the bias is.

We're too expensive for you — you'll never bias...

A good way to spot bias is when the writer presents their opinion as fact, e.g. by saying something confidently but giving no evidence for it. This weakens their argument, as you can claim all sorts of absurd things this way — only yesterday someone tried to tell me the moon's made of cheese.

Headlines and Subheadings

Presentational devices are used to make the page layout more interesting. You need to be able to say what specific <u>effects</u> they have. The beauty of them is that their effects are actually pretty obvious.

Headlines and Subheadings help organise the text

1) Headlines tell you <u>what</u> the article is <u>about</u>.

2) In newspapers and magazines, headlines are always <u>bigger</u> than the other words, and are at the <u>top</u> of the page.

3) Headlines capture your <u>interest</u>, so you'll read the article. They sometimes use <u>humour</u>, <u>exaggeration</u> or <u>shocking facts</u> to grab your attention.

1) <u>Subheadings</u> are used to <u>split</u> the story up into little pieces to make it look less daunting and <u>easier to read</u>.

2) Each subheading briefly tells you <u>what</u> the next section of text is about.

3) They're usually a bit <u>bigger</u> than the rest of the text and might be <u>bold</u> or <u>underlined</u> to make them stand out.

Headlines and Subheadings look like this

These bits are the headlines.

These are the subheadings.

CHANTELLE'S SECRET WEDDING SHOCKER

Private ceremony for TV's golden girl

By our showbiz reporter, Jane Snooping

Pop TV starlet Chantelle Williams has caused controversy by privately marrying her secret boyfriend Barry at a quiet ceremony in the Lake District.

CHANTELLE LOOKED BEAUTIFUL
According to insiders, the blonde bombshell was 'really excited' to be tying the knot with her childhood sweetheart. She looked beautiful in a traditional white laced gown and veil, carrying a bouquet of lilies.

Chantelle and Barry

FORMER BOYFRIEND IS 'APPALLED'
Former boyfriend and rock star, Parker, was apparently 'shocked and appalled' by the secret marriage. He refused to comment to The Daily Gossip, but insiders hinted that he was distraught.

COUPLE TO HONEYMOON IN CARIBBEAN
After their secret wedding, the couple jetted off on honeymoon to the beautiful island paradise of Antigua. They will stay at a luxury beach resort for two weeks before returning to London to set up their new home.

NEW BOATS KEEP FISHERMEN IN PLAICE

Hornsea fishermen are said to be 'overjoyed' at the gift of two wooden rowing boats from a local millionaire businessman and charity worker.

Sandy McTodd, 56, told The Daily Gossip, 'We love these boats - it's such a kind gift. Now we'll be able to row out to our hauler instead of swimming.'

residents were so excited about the new boats, and the prospect of ...sh for sale, that they held an all-night beach party with a giant bonfire ...ch revelry. 'This is the first good thing that's happened round here for ...ported Giles Hartley, an unemployed fishmonger.

...N PRESIDENT DECLARES WAR
...ws today, the American president has declared war on all countries ...nand over 'weapons of medium levels of destruction' in his ...r global submission. The UN is apparently 'quite worried'.

Write about headlines and subheadings Like This

The headline, "Chantelle's Secret Wedding Shocker", gets the reader's attention. It is short and hints at what the article will be about, making the reader want to find out more. For example, the word "secret" will interest readers because it implies that new information will be revealed.
    The subheadings guide the reader through the article, making it clear what each section is talking about. For example, the subheading "Couple to Honeymoon in Caribbean" tells the reader that the next paragraph is about the couple's honeymoon plans.

Don't forget to quote, even when it seems obvious.

Expand your point to show exactly what you mean.

Remember to explain why the technique is effective.

Subheadings — send in the substitute headteacher...

Headlines are there to attract your attention, so on some newspapers they're really big. If the headline's about something really exciting, it could be three inches tall — this makes it really stand out against its competitors on the newspaper stand when people are deciding which paper to buy.

Graphics and Captions

It's not only headlines and subheadings that make you want to start reading an article. Photos and captions are also used to grab the reader's <u>attention</u> — this page shows you how.

Graphics and Captions give us lots of Information

1) Texts often have graphics, e.g. photos or diagrams, to <u>illustrate</u> what they're about.

2) <u>Colourful graphics</u> can make the text look <u>more attractive</u> to the reader.

3) They usually have <u>captions</u> with them — a short bit of text to explain what the graphic shows.

4) Sometimes graphics are used to emphasise a <u>feeling</u> or <u>reinforce the message</u> of the text. For example, photos of the effects of war help us understand how <u>horrible</u> it must be.

5) Graphics can be specially <u>selected</u> or even <u>cropped</u> (cut or trimmed) to emphasise <u>one particular feeling</u> instead of others. E.g. a writer could make sure there are no <u>hopeful</u> photos of people being rescued in a war, that way we're <u>only shown</u> how horrible it is.

6) The reader can tell <u>what a text is about</u> just from a <u>quick glance</u> at the accompanying graphics.

Graphics and Captions look like this

Hurricane causes devastation

A lifetime of fun and affection — take me home

Friday, 9.00am

The photo shows more about the awful effects of the hurricane than the text alone could.

This picture is persuasive — the cute puppy is meant to make the reader feel a bit soppy.

The caption clarifies what's being shown — it tells you when the weather forecast is for.

Write about graphics and captions Like This

The photograph of the hurricane damage (shows us what the article is about,) even before we read any of the words. It is effective because (it is easy to understand quickly and makes us want to know more.) The photo also only shows the devastation — it doesn't show any of the buildings that are left standing or any signs of life. (This reinforces) the terrible impact of the hurricane.

The caption, "Hurricane causes devastation", tells us not only what happened, but also how we should feel about it. The word "devastation" in particular emphasises to the reader that the hurricane would have been a (horrendous experience for those involved.)

> State the purpose of the photo.

> Say why it's effective.

> Show how effective the caption is by describing its effect on the reader.

Aw, what a cute puppy...

Remember, the graphic always goes with the words in the article and is effective because it shows us what the article is about. Don't just say what the graphic is — say why it's effective and how it connects to the rest of the text. And remember to describe the emotional impact it has.

Text Boxes and Text Columns

Now you know how writers can grab your attention, you need to be able to talk about how they keep you interested. Text columns and boxes are two of their little ploys.

Boxes and Columns are ways of Presenting Text

1) Writers sometimes break their text up into columns — it makes it appear shorter and easier to read.

2) You see text columns all over the place — in magazines, newspapers, adverts etc.

1) Sometimes text is put in a box to grab your attention. The box can be made to stand out even more by making it a strong colour, or putting it at an angle.

2) Different sections can also be put in separate boxes to break up the main text and make it appear easier to read.

Text Columns and Text Boxes look like this

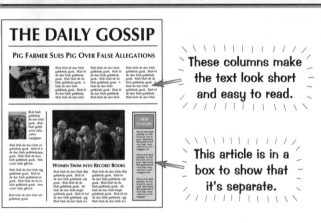

These columns make the text look short and easy to read.

This article is in a box to show that it's separate.

Brightly coloured and angled boxes make the text stand out.

Write about text columns and text boxes Like This

Columns have been used in the newspaper article to make the text easy to follow. The columns break down the long article about the pig farmer, making it appear shorter than if it was presented in a single block of text. This means that readers are not put off by the length of the article and will be more likely to read it.

In the magazine, text boxes have been used to make key pieces of information stand out. For example, the low price of the magazine has been highlighted in an eye-catching yellow box. This would attract a reader's attention and might persuade them to buy the magazine.

Show you know how the text columns work.

Remember to write about the effect these features are supposed to have on the reader.

Bruno and Tyson compete via mobile phone...

If you don't really get it, just think about a magazine without any columns or boxes. Imagine that all the writing just went from left to right in a giant block across the page. It'd be daunting to read — people would be scared away by the amount of text. Columns and boxes are clever little tricks really.

Bullet Points and Numbered Lists

Now that you understand how text boxes and text columns work, it's time to look at other devices that writers use to make sure their work is clearly presented and easy to understand.

Bullet Points **and** Numbered Lists **break texts down**

1) **Bullet points** are <u>dots</u>, <u>dashes</u> or other <u>symbols</u> that go at the start of each new point in a <u>list</u>.

2) Sometimes lists can be <u>numbered</u> instead.

3) Bullet points and numbered lists are often used when writers want to give you <u>lots of information</u>. They separate complex information into <u>step-by-step</u> points, to make it <u>easier to read</u>.

Bullet Points **and** Numbered Lists **look like this**

The scuba diving course covers:
- Equipment care
- Breathing from a regulator
- Swimming easily underwater
- Caring for the environment
- Being safe

Before your exam make sure that you:
1. Know where and when the exam is.
2. Get a good night's sleep.
3. Wake up in time to have breakfast.
4. Have everything you need for the exam.

I'm sure there wa something I had t do today...

Tracy had forgotten point 5 — do the exam.

Dots are used as bullet points.

These points give you information.

This is a numbered list.

These points give you advice.

Write **about bullet points and numbered lists** Like This

Show you know that the writer has thought carefully about how to present the text.

Show you understand that the numbers are there for a reason.

The writer has chosen to summarise what you might learn in a scuba diving course by using bullet points. This is an effective way of presenting a large amount of information, as it breaks the points down, making them easier to follow. Without the bullet points, there would seem to be a lot of text to sift through before the reader gets to what they need.

　　In the second example, the writer presents his advice as a numbered list. The use of numbers emphasises the order in which the advice should be followed. It also reassures the reader by giving the impression that there is only a limited amount of information to remember.

Show you know that bullet points have an effect on the reader.

My bullet points didn't work — they must've been blanks...

OK, it doesn't take a genius to spot a bullet point, but it's still worth writing about them. Show the examiner that you understand the effect different ways of presenting text can have on the reader. You might get yourself a couple of extra marks — which is always nice.

Font Styles and Formatting

You need to remember that everything on a page tells you something about the text. This includes what the writing looks like.

Fonts are different *Styles* of printed text

1) The <u>font</u> of a text gives you a clue about <u>what kind</u> of text it is.

2) Serious, formal fonts are for <u>serious</u>, formal texts.

3) Cartoony, informal fonts are for <u>light-hearted</u> texts, or texts for <u>children</u>.

Fonts can be <u>formatted</u>, e.g. by making them **bold** or *italic*, <u>underlining</u> them or putting them in CAPITALS.

Writers format fonts to <u>emphasise</u> particular words or phrases and make them really <u>stand out</u>.

The mischievous smile meant she'd written her speech in Litterbox ICG again.

Here are some examples of *Different Fonts*

This font is formal and sets a serious tone. It could be used for newspaper articles.

This font is informal and easy to read. It could be used for children's books.

This font looks quirky and old-fashioned. It could be used for wedding invitations.

Font Formatting *looks like this*

WOMEN SWIM INTO RECORD BOOKS

At 10pm last night, the last of the **5,000** female swimmers arrived at Calais, having set off from Dover at 5am. This marks the largest group swim ever in the history of swimming.

The women together have raised over **a million pounds** for a variety of charities. They plan to repeat the event next year, and hopefully will double their numbers.

The event's organiser, Gill Potts, said, *"I'm really pleased with everyone's effort. They had to swim through two miles of jellyfish, but not one of them complained."*

Waiting at Calais was Robbie Williams, who had promised a **kiss** for each swimmer to arrive. When told that 5,000 women were approaching the shore, the singer was apparently *"a little shocked"*.

Could <u>you</u> swim the channel? Visit <u>www.swimmingisgreat.uk.png</u> for details on next year's event.

Bold is useful for highlighting important words.

Underlining can also be used to highlight important words.

Capital letters are often used for headings.

Italics can be used to highlight quotes.

Write about fonts *Like This*

The newspaper article uses a formal font. This creates a serious tone appropriate for a news article. The font is clear and easy to read, making the long article less intimidating to the reader.

One of the writer's intentions is to make the readers realise how many people took part in the swim, and how much money they raised. This is made really clear as "5,000" and "a million pounds" are printed in bold, making these words stand out from the rest.

You don't need to know the names of the fonts — just describe them.

Remember to explain the effect of the formatting.

I'd like to do some formatting, if I may be so bold...

Remember, the font tells you about the tone of the text at first glance. So a serious, boring font tells you that the text is probably very formal and is not a laughing matter. A silly, cartoony font tells you that the text is light-hearted, jokey and informal. It's not rocket science, this font stuff.

Descriptive Language

The texts you have to write about in the exam will use lots of different language techniques to make them more effective. You need to be able to recognise the techniques and say why they're used.

Descriptive Language makes text Interesting

1) Writers use descriptive techniques so that the reader gets a really clear <u>image</u> in their head of what the writer's describing. It makes the text more <u>interesting</u>, <u>dramatic</u> and <u>real</u>.

2) <u>Descriptive language</u> includes <u>imagery</u> such as metaphors, similes and personification. (See pages 25-26 for more on these.)

3) Writers often give <u>descriptions</u> based on their five <u>senses</u> (what they can <u>see</u>, <u>smell</u>, <u>hear</u>, <u>touch</u> or <u>taste</u>).

4) Another sign of descriptive language is when the writer uses lots of <u>adjectives</u> — describing words like "huge" or "fiery" that give a specific <u>impression</u> of something. This technique is known as <u>story-telling style</u>.

Rex could think of plenty of words to describe what he'd just heard.

> **EXAMPLE**   After the dreary, grey sheet of rain had swept over the land, the parched, sun-baked fields transformed into a fertile, emerald-green valley.

5) Writers can also <u>build up</u> the description of something <u>throughout</u> their work. For example, they might do this by writing sentences with <u>contrasting</u> descriptions or descriptions that <u>agree</u> with each other. That way, <u>more detail</u> is added to the description as you read each sentence.

6) The way a piece of writing is <u>structured</u> can also help to develop description. Lots of <u>simple</u>, <u>short</u> sentences create a <u>fast-paced</u>, <u>exciting</u> description. <u>Longer</u>, more <u>complicated</u> sentences mean descriptions are built up <u>slowly</u>, more <u>gently</u> and with <u>lots of detail</u>.

Write about descriptive language Like This

Here are your <u>examples</u>.

Describe any <u>techniques</u> that the writer has used to build up the description.

> The writer uses descriptive language to show the effect of the rain on the African landscape. In the first part of the sentence he uses adjectives such as "dreary" and "grey" to describe the rain. This creates a downbeat, unhappy image. He reinforces this impression by going on to describe the land as being "parched" and the fields "sun-baked". The writer then contrasts these images with the "fertile, emerald-green valley" that has been created. This allows the reader to picture in his or her own mind just how dramatic the changes that the rains bring are. Perhaps the writer is trying to show, through the contrast of negative images with positive images, that the time after the rains are a time of great joy.

<u>Explain</u> why the writer has used descriptive language.

<u>Develop</u> your point, e.g. say what you think the writer's <u>intention</u> is.

To get the marks, you need to <u>examine</u> the use of descriptive language — say <u>why</u> you think it makes the text more interesting for the reader.

My dad used descriptive language when I broke his mug...

It's not too hard to get the hang of writing about these techniques — just spot where one's been used, quote it, and explain how it's been used deliberately to affect the reader in some way. Easy.

Metaphors and Similes

Metaphors and similes are both types of <u>imagery</u>. They're different ways of <u>comparing</u> things.

Metaphors and similes are Comparisons

Metaphors and similes describe one thing by <u>comparing</u> it to something else. Writers use them to create a <u>picture</u> in the <u>reader's mind</u>.

> <u>Metaphors</u> describe something by saying that it <u>is</u> something else.

EXAMPLE Suddenly we were in the middle of the war zone. I tried to run but my feet <u>were</u> blocks of concrete.

> <u>Similes</u> describe something by saying that it's <u>like</u> something else. They usually use the words <u>as</u> or <u>like</u>.

EXAMPLE Sitting on my balcony, the humid Italian air clings to my skin <u>like</u> a warm, wet blanket.

Write about metaphors Like This

Here's your point, made right at the start of your paragraph.

Here's your explanation.

The journalist uses a metaphor when reporting from the war zone, "I tried to run but my feet were blocks of concrete". This shows that he was paralysed with fear and was unable to flee, which gives the reader a sense of the reporter's panic at being in such a frightening situation. I think the use of this metaphor makes the description really effective because it helps the readers to empathise with the journalist.

Here's your example.

Here's where you develop your point.

Write about similes Like This

This quote is tucked neatly into the sentence. Examiners love embedded quotations like this.

The writer uses a simile when describing the humid weather in Italy. By comparing the air to a "warm, wet blanket", the reader can really feel just how unpleasantly damp and sticky the air is.

Don't do it like this

This is too general. Write about <u>one</u> of the metaphors or similes in particular.

The writer uses lots of metaphors and similes which make the text more interesting.

Don't just say they make it more interesting. To get the marks, you need to say <u>why</u> they make the text more interesting for the reader.

The spectre of the exam lurked like an invisible tiger...

Metaphors — his breath was ice, my boss is a pussycat really, your trainers are pure cheese.
Similes — his breath was as cold as ice, my boss is as nice as a cat, your trainers smell like cheese.

Analogy and Personification

Analogy, personification — too many new words? Sorry about that...

Analogies are just fancy Comparisons

An analogy is a kind of extended simile (see page 25 for more on similes).
The writer simply compares two different things to explain what they're saying and make it clearer.

> **EXAMPLES**
> Hoping your exams will go OK without opening your books is like hoping for a win on the lottery without ever buying a ticket.
>
> Deforestation is happening at an incredible speed. An area of rainforest equal to twenty football pitches is lost every minute.

Write about analogies Like This

Here's your example.

Try to make your point in the first sentence.

Develop your point — say why the writer wants to affect the reader in this way.

Explain the effect of the analogy on the reader.

To help him explain about deforestation, the writer uses an analogy when he says that, "An area of rainforest equal to twenty football pitches is lost every minute." This allows the audience to understand the phenomenal speed of this destruction, by making a comparison which they can easily visualise. The use of this analogy increases the impact that the information has on the reader, making the writer's argument more persuasive.

Personification is describing a thing as a Person

1) Personification means describing something as if it's a person, or sometimes an animal — in the way it looks, moves, sounds or some other aspect of it.

2) Personification makes descriptions seem to "come to life".

3) It can also help to give a sense of how the writer feels about something.

> **EXAMPLE**   Military helicopters prowl the city, their menacing mechanical voices threatening to destroy any sign of activity.

Write about personification Like This

Say what impression the personification creates.

As always, give examples.

Develop your idea.

The writer's use of personification makes the helicopters appear threatening and dangerous. She describes how they "prowl the city", making it appear to be the helicopters themselves who are in charge, rather than the people controlling them. The "menacing mechanical voices" add to the impression of a frightening, evil force controlling the city. The writer is implying that the military helicopters are not a positive presence. I think she strongly disapproves of the military presence in the city.

I hate comparing — I've got analogy to it...

Simply spotting that a writer has used a technique isn't enough — you need to explain the purpose of the technique and why it's effective. It's about showing you understand what the writer is up to.

Alliteration and Onomatopoeia

Writers use lots of different techniques to stop their readers getting bored.
Alliteration and onomatopoeia are used as sound effects in writing to keep readers interested.

Alliteration means repeating the same Sound

Alliteration is when words that are close together begin with the same sound. It makes
the sentence seem more interesting to the reader. Alliteration is often found in headlines:

P.M.'s Panic

Rooney Rules the Roost

Close Call for Kids

Magic Murray Marches on

In the exam you'll need to be able to identify alliteration and write about how and why it's been used.

Write about alliteration Like This

Here's your point, right in the first sentence.

Here's an example.

By using the alliteration of "Magic Murray Marches on", the writer attracts the reader's attention to the article on Andy Murray at Wimbledon. Alliteration emphasises the headline and gives the article a snappy, easy-to-read opening which encourages readers to continue.

Explain why the writer has used alliteration...

...and develop your point.

Onomatopoeia means using words that Imitate Noises

Onomatopoeia means using words that sound like the noises being described. This makes
the description of the sounds more vivid to the reader. Here are some good examples:

Thud   Slurp   Crackle   Smash   Tinkle   Screech   Hiss   Squish

Write about onomatopoeia Like This

Remember the effect on the reader.

Here's the example.

Including the onomatopoeic word "slurp" in the cartoon used in the milkshake advertisement makes the audience recognise the humorous noise often made by children when they drink. The advert is aimed at children, so this helps them to identify with the cartoon character and makes the product more appealing for them.

Think about the purpose of the text when you're writing about onomatopoeia.

Onomatopoeia — what a stupid word...

Learn how to spell ON-O-MAT-O-POEI-A. You'll impress the examiner if you can spell it correctly.
It's hard, I know, but just write it out a few times and you'll get the hang of it eventually.

Irony and Sarcasm

Irony and sarcasm are techniques that are related to the <u>tone</u> of the writing (see glossary).

Irony *is saying the* Opposite *of what you* Mean

1) <u>Irony</u> is when the <u>literal meaning</u> of a piece of writing is the exact <u>opposite</u> of its <u>intended meani</u>
2) The reader can tell the writer is being ironic from the context of the writing.
3) Irony is often <u>humorous</u> or <u>light-hearted</u>.

EXAMPLE We were stranded at the airport for 48 hours with no food, which was just great.

Of course, the writer doesn't <u>really</u> mean it was great. In fact, he means it was the <u>opposite</u> of great.

Write *about irony Like This*

Here's your point. Say <u>why</u> the writer has used irony.

Here's your evidence.

The writer uses irony to express his frustration at having his flight delayed for two days. When he says that being there for 48 hours with no food was "just great" he actually means the opposite — that it was a depressing and annoying experience. He is using irony to amuse the reader, whilst also making them feel sympathetic towards him.

Here's your explanation.

Here's where you develop your point.

Sarcasm *is* Nastier *than irony*

1) The word "<u>sarcasm</u>" comes from a Greek word that literally means "<u>flesh tearing</u>".
2) <u>Sarcasm</u> is language that has a <u>mocking</u> or <u>scornful</u> tone. It's often intended to <u>insult someone</u> or <u>make fun</u> of them, or to show that the writer is <u>angry</u> or <u>annoyed</u> about something.
3) Sarcastic writing often uses <u>irony</u> — but the tone is more <u>aggressive</u> and <u>unpleasant</u>.

EXAMPLE The council's latest brainwave on tackling petty crime is to take away the few local facilities available to youngsters. This is presumably intended to encourage them to stay indoors watching Hollyoaks rather than engaging with society in any way.

Write *about sarcasm Like This*

The writer's use of sarcasm in describing the council's "brainwave" shows how stupid he thinks the scheme is. His sarcastic comment that it is "presumably intended" to exclude young people from society suggests that the council have not thought it through. Rather than being a clever way of reducing crime, he clearly believes it will make the problem worse.

Show the intended effect of the sarcasm.

Say what the writer is implying, and how it adds to their argument.

Sarcasm, yeah right, what a great technique...

One kind of text that often uses irony and sarcasm is <u>satire</u>. Satire is designed to make fun out of a particular person or thing. Satirical texts are often political, with the intention of ruining the reputation of a politician or government by imitating them but emphasising their bad points.

Technical and Emotive Language

Some of the texts in the exam might use technical language to sound knowledgeable and add detail. Others may use more emotive language to try to persuade you to take their point of view.

Technical language is often used to Support an argument

1) <u>Technical</u> language includes things like <u>specialist terms</u>, <u>jargon</u> and <u>statistics</u>. It gives an impression of the writer having <u>in-depth knowledge</u> of the topic they're writing about.

2) You'll find technical language in textbooks, instructions, reports, and even newspaper articles.

3) It's often used to present facts to <u>support</u> an argument, making it more <u>convincing</u> to the reader.

> **EXAMPLE** Governments need to act now to combat climate change. Average worldwide temperatures have increased by about 1°C in the last hundred years, mainly due to increased emission of greenhouse gases such as carbon dioxide and methane.

Write about technical language Like This

Describe the impression the technical details create.

By including technical terms relating to climate change, such as "Average worldwide temperatures" and "greenhouse gases", the writer gives the impression that he understands the finer details of the issue. This implication supports his argument that governments need to take more action to deal with climate change.

Say how it helps the writer's argument.

Emotive language is used to Persuade

1) Writers use emotive language to get the reader to <u>feel</u> really <u>strongly</u> about something. This could be feelings of disgust, sadness, happiness, anger or any other <u>emotion</u>.

2) Language is often made emotive by <u>strong adjectives</u>, e.g. "shocking", "shameful" or "heroic".

3) <u>Emotive</u> language can <u>emphasise</u> a point — it usually makes the <u>writer's opinion</u> very clear.

> **EXAMPLE** The bears are forced to perform these painful dances and are frequently subjected to physical abuse.

Write about emotive language Like This

Say how the emotive language is used.

The leaflet against animal cruelty uses highly emotive language. The words "forced" and "painful" are used to manipulate the reader's response, persuading them to feel, as the writer does, that this treatment is inhumane and unjustifiable.

Talk about the overall effect on the reader.

Here comes the science...

Two more types of language to learn here, but nothing too hard to get your head around. Technical language can be used to give detail, but more often than not it's there to make the author sound like they know what they're on about. And emotive language makes you emotional. Tricky eh?

Structure

"Structure" means the way different parts of a text are put together. These examples are all from newspaper articles, but the same trends tend to occur in other non-fiction texts.

Introductions create Interest in the text

1) An introduction should briefly give the reader the main points of the article.
2) It should also try to capture the reader's interest so that they read the rest of the article.

e.g. Fears were voiced last night for the safety of the lone whale who was spotted in the Thames by the Embankment in Central London. Onlookers have nicknamed him "Fred" and have taken to the banks of the river to watch. Marine biologists are on hand to oversee the task of returning "Fred" to the wild.

Unusual information and emotive words make the reader want to find out more.

Gives the reader the main points.

Write about introductions Like This

Make your point straight away.

The introduction of this text is effective because of the tone and the language used. The emotive words in the first sentence, such as "Fears", "safety" and "lone", immediately interest the reader. In addition, the introduction gives the main points of the article so that the reader can understand what it is about as well as deciding whether to read on.

Show that you understand the key purposes of the introduction.

Here are some good examples.

The middle tells you Who, What, Where, When and Why

After the introduction, the main bit of text gives the answers to all the questions that readers might want to ask — who, what, where, when and why.

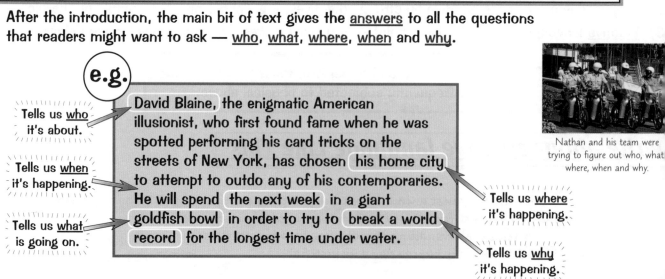

e.g.

Tells us who it's about.

Tells us when it's happening.

Tells us what is going on.

David Blaine, the enigmatic American illusionist, who first found fame when he was spotted performing his card tricks on the streets of New York, has chosen his home city to attempt to outdo any of his contemporaries. He will spend the next week in a giant goldfish bowl in order to try to break a world record for the longest time under water.

Tells us where it's happening.

Tells us why it's happening.

Nathan and his team were trying to figure out who, what where, when and why.

Who? What? Where? Nurse, the pills...

This is all fairly obvious really — the introduction gives a general idea of what's in the article, then you get the details. The next page shows you how these details are structured in the main text, before it's all nicely summed up in the conclusion. And they all lived happily ever after...

Structure

Let's face it, an article full of random info would be pretty hard to read. Which is why most articles link it all together into a neat little package.

The Body of the text is usually Structured in Paragraphs

Here's one common way of structuring an article:

1) The <u>main points</u> of a text are first given very briefly in the <u>introduction</u>.

2) Each <u>paragraph</u> of the <u>main body</u> of the text then <u>expands</u> on these ideas in turn.

Here's the main body of the whale article from the previous page:

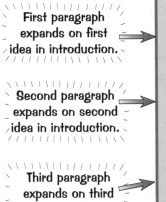

First paragraph expands on first idea in introduction.

Second paragraph expands on second idea in introduction.

Third paragraph expands on third idea in introduction.

> The whale, identified as a humpback that would normally be found in transatlantic waters, is bleeding from a wound to its side. It has been swimming alongside the Houses of Parliament all afternoon, having first been spotted by a French tourist who was walking the popular route.
>
> The number of onlookers has rapidly increased during the afternoon as news of Fred's sighting spread through the cafes, shops and offices of Central London. An unconfirmed source has reported that the Prime Minister has been informed and is being kept up to date with the unusual event. The crowd has also been very considerate of the whale's welfare by maintaining a quiet presence.
>
> Experts on marine biology arrived at the scene shortly after midday with a mass of equipment designed to measure and constantly record Fred's heart and stress rates. Dr John Tweed from University College commented on his fears for the safety of the whale because of his injuries and the amount of blood he has lost. He stated that his main priority was to return "Fred" to the open sea.

Conclusions summarise the Main Points

1) Conclusions give a <u>summary</u> of the <u>main points</u> of an article.

2) To be effective, they should leave the reader <u>thinking</u> about the <u>subject</u> of the article.

This summarises what was in the text.

This makes the reader think about their own attitudes.

> The questions that remain unanswered are how "Fred" came to be in the Thames and whether or not he will die, confirming the worst fears of most experts. However, the most intriguing question is why are we, as humans, so interested in his plight?

Write about conclusions Like This

Show that you understand that conclusions sum things up and remind the reader of the key points.

Show how the conclusion helps the reader to engage with the text.

> The conclusion sums up the main points of the article such as the views of the experts and their concerns that Fred will not survive. This ensures that the reader recalls the important details in the text.
> In addition, the last sentence, which asks the question as to why humans are so interested, encourages the reader to examine his or her own feelings on the subject.

And in conclusion, this is all dead easy...

So let me get this straight — the introduction's at the start and the conclusion's at the end, you say? You're absolutely sure about that then? Well, it's crazy, but it just might work...

Search and Find Questions

The simplest type of exam question asks you to pick out particular information from a text. Examiners call these "search and find" questions. Here are some tips on how to answer them well...

Some questions ask you to Pick Out Information

1) These questions test your ability to <u>understand</u> and <u>interpret</u> the text, <u>select</u> relevant <u>information</u> and <u>order</u> it into a <u>coherent</u> answer.

2) Here's an example:

> **Look at Betty Munro's newspaper article 'Homecoming'.**
>
> **1.** According to Betty Munro, why is the town of Melrose a wonderful place to live? You must use the text to support your answer.
>
> [10 marks]

3) This type of question is fairly straightforward — but you need to make sure you find <u>all</u> the <u>relevant details</u> and write about them <u>clearly</u> to get <u>top marks</u>.

Read the text Carefully

1) After you've read the exam question, <u>look back through</u> the <u>text</u> (some questions tell you to only look at <u>certain paragraphs</u> or <u>line numbers</u>).

2) As you read, <u>underline</u> information that <u>answers the question</u>. E.g. here's part of the text that goes with the exam question above:

> At the age of 46, I was fed up of London. I sold my house and rented a cottage in the <u>idyllic</u> Scottish town where I grew up. After just a few weeks, I knew I'd made the right decision: Melrose, with its <u>friendly people</u> and <u>stunning scenery</u>, is where my heart is and it's a wonderful place to live.
>
> It is <u>terribly pretty</u>, with the kind of <u>charming, local shops</u> that are rapidly being replaced by supermarket giants elsewhere. For such a tiny place, it is <u>buzzing with life</u>. There's a <u>theatre</u>, <u>museum</u> and literary society. The <u>sporting facilities</u> are fantastic, with an <u>excellent rugby pitch</u>.

It's important to Keep your answer Focused

1) Select the parts of the text that <u>answer the question best</u> — don't include any extra waffle.

2) You can use <u>short quotes</u>, or explain what the writer says <u>in your own words</u>. If you use quotes, remember to use <u>quotation marks</u>.

3) Avoid quoting <u>long chunks</u> — it gives the examiner the impression that you <u>don't understand</u> the text and can't tell which bits are most important.

4) All the points you make should be <u>based on the text</u> and <u>help to answer the question</u>.

THIS WOULD BE GOOD:	THIS WOULD BE BAD:
The writer says Melrose is "terribly pretty" and has "charming" shops. She is also enthusiastic about the sporting facilities, for example the "excellent" rugby field.	The writer says that at the age of 46, she was fed up with London. She must have been bored with cities. She seems to think Melrose is much better than London, probably because it's rural.

Where could you find a question? — Search me....

With 'search and find' questions it's important to follow the text closely, and pick out all the relevant points. Don't get sidetracked. Save your skills of insight and evaluation for the trickier questions...

P.E.E.D.

For some of the <u>trickier questions</u>, you've got to "<u>explain and evaluate</u>" how writers try to <u>influence</u> their readers. For these questions, <u>P.E.E.D.</u> is a pretty nifty technique.

P.E.E.D. stands for Point, Example, Explain, Develop

P.E.E.D. helps you <u>structure</u> your answers to those trickier questions:

1) Make a <u>point</u> to answer the question you've been given.

2) Then give an <u>example</u> from the text (either a quote or a description).

3) After that, <u>explain</u> how your example backs up your point.

4) Finally, <u>develop</u> your point — this might involve saying what the <u>effect on the reader</u> is, saying what the <u>writer's intention</u> is, <u>linking</u> your point to another part of the text or giving your <u>own opinion</u>.

> You don't need to use P.E.E.D. for all your answers — if the question just asks you to find some information, then you don't need to explain or develop your points.

There's more about how to do this on page 35.

Here's an example answer that includes those <u>four</u> things:

This is your <u>point</u>.

This bit is your <u>explanation</u>.

> The writer feels quite angry about school dinners. She says school food is "pallid, tasteless pap". The word "pap" has a disgusted sound to it. It emphasises how appalled she is at the low quality of the food. I think the writer's intention is to show that it isn't surprising that school dinners are unpopular. She is implying that schools should provide food that isn't disgusting if they want children to eat it.

This is your <u>example</u>.

This is where you <u>develop</u> your point further.

Explain what your example Shows about the Text

1) Your example will usually be a <u>quote</u>, but it can also be a <u>reference</u>, e.g. a description of the pictures, font, layout or structure of the text. That's fine. It still counts as the example bit.

2) The <u>explanation</u> and <u>development</u> parts are very important. They're your chance to show that you <u>really understand</u> and have <u>thought about</u> the text.

Here are some answers with different types of <u>examples</u> and <u>well-developed</u> points:

This <u>example</u> mentions <u>text appearance</u>.

This bit <u>develops</u> the point — it says what the <u>writer's intention</u> is.

> The design of this leaflet will appeal to children. For example, it uses primary colours and simple fonts, which give a friendly, unsophisticated impression. The writer's intention is to make the leaflet seem easy to read and understand. Children won't be put off by the appearance of the leaflet, so they'll be more likely to read the leaflet and learn from it.

This <u>explains</u> why this <u>style of presentation</u> would appeal to children.

This bit <u>develops</u> the point further — it says <u>what effect</u> the leaflet will have on children.

A <u>language device</u> is the <u>example</u> here.

This <u>develops</u> the point further.

> The writer sounds as if he is confused. For example, he starts each paragraph with a question, giving the impression that he doesn't understand what's happening to him. This is reinforced by the worried-looking photograph of him at the top of the page. The writer's confusion creates a sense of unease in the reader, leading them to question their own understanding of the issue.

This <u>explanation</u> links with another part of the text.

Would you like to share the joke with the rest of the class?

P.E.E.D. is a good way of improving your answers to the slightly harder questions. So, for the more in-depth exam questions, remember to check you've P.E.E.D. on your work (sorry, couldn't resist).

Writing in Paragraphs

I'm sure you know about paragraphs already so I'm not going to go on about <u>how</u> to write in paragraphs. But you do need to know <u>why</u> it's so important.

Paragraphs are a good way to Structure Your Answer

1) You need to <u>organise</u> your points clearly and <u>link</u> them together
— and the best way to do that is to write in <u>paragraphs</u>.

2) You can use different paragraph <u>structures</u> to organise your points in <u>different ways</u>.
For example:

- You could write a paragraph for <u>every point</u> you want to make, and each paragraph could have a <u>P.E.E.D. structure</u> (see previous page).
- You could make <u>two points</u> that <u>contrast</u> or <u>agree with</u> each other within a paragraph — this can be useful when <u>comparing</u> two texts (see page 37).
- You could make <u>one point</u> and link together <u>lots of examples</u> with <u>different explanations</u> within a paragraph.

How you Start each New Paragraph is important

<u>Linking</u> your paragraphs together smoothly is an important skill — it makes your writing look <u>more confident</u> and <u>better thought out</u>.

1) **The beginning of a paragraph needs to show <u>what</u> the paragraph is <u>about</u>. Link it to <u>key words</u> in the question.**

> The writer creates an immediate sense of anger through the headlines she chooses.

This makes it clear you're answering a question about how the writer shows anger.

2) **You might want to <u>link</u> a new point with a <u>previous paragraph</u>.**

> This is not the only way in which the writer shows bias.

This refers back to the paragraph you've just finished.

3) **You could show you're <u>moving on</u> to another topic.**

> The writer's choice of fonts is also important.

This introduces your new topic.

4) **You might be introducing a <u>comparison</u> or <u>contrast</u> within a text.**

> Although the first paragraph uses lots of questions, the rest of the article sounds much more definite.

This word helps you start writing about a difference.

See page 11 for some more examples of linking words and phrases.

Make a chart of tropical birds — draw a parrotgraph...

This stuff kind of comes naturally when you've had enough practice. So keep doing practice exams and answering practice questions — pretty soon you'll be producing beautiful answers.

Reading with Insight

Reading with insight is what the examiners call a 'higher order' reading skill. That means you've got to show you can do it to get the higher grades — especially when you're asked to discuss or comment.

You need to look Beyond what's Obvious

Reading with insight helps you to <u>develop</u> your points — that's the 'D' in P.E.E.D. (see p.33).

You may understand the facts a writer gives you, but you'll need to write about <u>more</u> than just those facts for some of your answers.

1) You can show <u>insight</u> if you work out what a writer's <u>attitude</u> is. For example:

> There is a strong sense that the writer feels angry about the changes.

2) You could show you understand <u>what</u> the writer wants readers to <u>think about</u>. For example:

> The article makes the reader question whether schools are a good thing.

3) You could comment on how the writer tries to make readers <u>feel</u>. For example:

> The writer seems to want to make readers feel guilty.

4) You might write about <u>why</u> you think a piece was written. For example:

> Perhaps the writer felt he needed to make sure the memory of his friend was kept alive.

5) You could comment on any <u>changes</u> to the writer's <u>argument</u> or <u>language style</u> within the text. For example:

> The writer uses a serious, formal tone to describe the new exam rules, but then changes to a more informal, light-hearted style to wish students good luck in their exams.

The Examiner wants to hear Your Opinion

You can get marks for giving a thoughtful <u>personal response</u>. Make sure you focus on the <u>text</u> though — examiners don't want to know your general opinions on various unrelated issues.

THIS WOULD BE GOOD:

> I think the article would remind older people of happier times because it includes so many descriptive details.

THIS WOULD BE BAD:

> I think old people are quite boring.

Examiners love Alternative Interpretations

If you give <u>more than one</u> possible way of <u>looking</u> at a text, the examiner will be extremely impressed. For example:

> The short sentences could give an impression of anxiety and tension, or they could suggest to some readers that the writer has an arrogant attitude.

This shows that you've got plenty of ideas.

Make sure you're reading with insight of a cup of tea...

There's lots of really good advice on this page. I'd read it over one more time if I were you. You've got to show some insight, give your opinion and give different interpretations, if you can.

Reading with Insight

If you're after those high grades, you've got to go a bit further than finding facts. You'll need to work out what writers are <u>implying</u> too. This is where <u>inference</u> and <u>empathy</u> come in.

Inference means working things out from Clues

Writers don't always make things obvious. You can use <u>evidence</u> in the text to work out what the writer <u>really</u> wants us to think. Make sure you use <u>details</u> from the text though. Don't just guess.

1) <u>Language</u> gives you clues.

> The writer uses words like "endless" and "unoriginal", which imply that he did not enjoy the film.

This shows you have made an inference.

2) You can draw inferences from <u>pictures</u>.

> The article appears to be critical of the circus because it includes pictures of cramped animal cages and fields full of litter.

You can use this phrase to infer too.

3) Text <u>details</u> give you hints.

> The writer gives a sense of being biased in favour of the exam system because she only uses examples of successful candidates.

This phrase introduces another inference.

It's useful to work out the Writer's Tone

Obviously, you can't actually hear the writer's tone of voice. But the <u>language</u> in the text can give away the writer's <u>emotions</u> and <u>attitudes</u> — and that's called <u>tone</u> too.

Here's an answer that mentions the writer's <u>tone</u>:

> The writer sounds sarcastic when she calls the contestants "the finest brains the country could scrape together."

This bit comments on tone.

See p.9-10 and p.28 for more on tone.

You can Show Empathy with the writer

1) Empathy means showing you <u>understand</u> how the writer <u>feels</u>.
2) You could make a <u>link</u> between the <u>writer's experiences</u> and <u>your own</u>.
3) <u>Don't</u> give too much <u>detail</u> about yourself though. The examiner's only interested in your understanding of the <u>text</u> — not your life story.

Here's a good example:

Sandra preferred to show empathy with dolphins.

Use phrases like this to show empathy.

> The writer seems to be anxious and restless, just like I would feel before an exam.
> It must have been uncomfortable for him.

He snored loudly, giving the sense that he was bored...

Don't worry if some of these techniques sound a bit tricky. There are lots of different ways to show insight. Most questions have more than one right answer — that's what makes English such fun...

Comparing Texts

In the exam, there's usually a question that asks you about both texts. You might have to compare what the writers say, or what they think about something in particular. These questions can be tricky — so here's a page of hints about how to tackle them...

Quickly Plan your answer Before you start Writing

Here's a question that asks you to compare two texts:

> 4. Compare and contrast the two texts, *Teen Times* and *Youth Out of Control*, using the following headings:
>
> - the writers' intended audiences;
> - the ways in which the writers talk about young people.
>
> [10 marks]

Set your notes out in lists, side by side, to help you compare.

And here's how you could quickly plan an answer to that question:

Each set of notes matches a bullet point in the question.

Teen Times
- Audience — teenagers, because it uses informal font, cartoons
- Way they talk about young people — examples of achievements, inclusive tone, use of first person

Youth Out of Control
- Audience — adult readers, because it uses columns, small font
- Way they talk about young people — examples of bad behaviour, sarcastic tone, use of third person

Write an Equal Amount about Each Text

Here's part of a possible answer to the question above:

This introduces a difference.

This introduces your example.

This is the explanation bit.

Intended audience
The author of 'Teen Times' is writing for a teenage audience, whereas 'Youth Out of Control' is for a general adult readership. This is partly suggested by the appearance of each text. The first text uses an informal looking font and illustrates the piece with cartoons, creating a sense of youth and energy. The second text, on the other hand, is set out in traditional newspaper columns with a small font size, which suggests that it is aimed at adults.

How they write about young people
Although both pieces are about teenagers, the texts differ in the way they refer to young people; the subheadings in the first text use the first person ("we"), while the second text refers to teenagers in the third person ("they"). This shows that 'Teen Times' tries to identify with youngsters, while 'Youth Out of Control' does not.

This points out a similarity.

Here's another difference.

Next up, all the way from Bolton — oh you said "compare"...

Questions about two texts will sometimes give you bullet points for guidance. Make sure you cover all of these bullet points in your answer — otherwise you'll lose out on marks.

Other Question Types

Just when you thought it was all over, along I come with yet more question types. Sigh.

You could be asked what Impression a text gives you

1) You could be asked to explain what impression you get of the writer or the things they've written about, e.g. the writer is very happy, the text is about a very successful company.
2) The question might also ask what image the text creates, e.g. what image does this text create of the writer? This is the same thing as the impression it creates.

Think about what you've learnt about Bob Brown from the text.

> 1. What impression do you get of the writer, Bob Brown?   [10 marks]

Viewpoint/Attitude questions ask what the Writer Thinks

1) You might be asked to work out what a writer's attitude, opinions, viewpoint or thoughts and feelings on a subject are.
2) For any of these you basically just have to pick out what the writer thinks, e.g. the writer's opinion of the car is that it is ugly.

> 1. What are the writer's opinions of Burnley town centre?
> [10 marks]

You only need to write about his opinions of Burnley town centre — don't write about what he thinks of anything else.

Intended Audience questions ask Who the text is Aimed at

1) You might have to work out which group of people the writer wants to read their text, e.g. children, dog owners or teachers (see p.2 for more on audience).
2) You'll usually need to explain your reasons for saying who the text is aimed at as well.

Write about how each of these things show who the text is aimed at.

> 1. Who is the leaflet aimed at? Think about:
> • what it says;
> • how it says it.   [10 marks]

You could also be asked about things like how the text is organised or the use of presentational features.

You could also be asked to Analyse Persuasive Techniques

1) Some questions ask you to spot the techniques that writers use to keep readers interested, to argue a point or to persuade them to do something.
2) Sometimes you'll be given bullet points that tell you what to write about for these questions. If you aren't, you should always think about what the text says, how it says it, how the text is organised and how the article has been presented.

> 1. How does the writer try to encourage you to visit Italy?   [10 marks]

You need to pick out specific techniques like language and the pictures that have been used.

I have a question — can I stop revising now?

Sadly, I'm afraid the answer to that one is 'no'. But on the plus side, you're now into the exam section of the book, where you get to practise some sample exam questions. Woop woop.

Summary of the Exam

bet you're just aching to know all about your exams. Well, the next two pages tell you what he examiners have got in store for you and give you some tips on how to keep them happy.

Each Exam Lasts for One Hour

1) Whether you're doing <u>GCSE English Language</u> or <u>GCSE English</u>, you have to do <u>two exams</u>.

2) They're the <u>same</u> exams for both courses, and they cover <u>Unit 1: Reading: non-fiction texts</u> and <u>Unit 2: Writing: information and ideas</u>.

3) You get <u>one hour</u> for each exam.

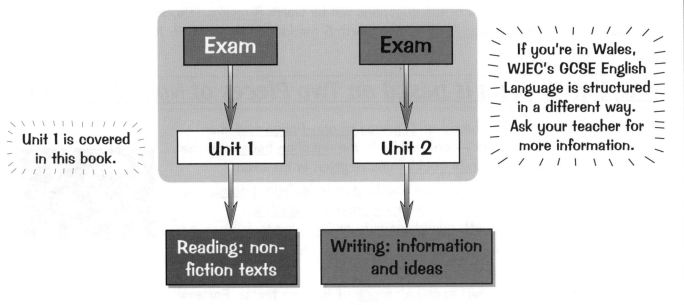

Unit 1 is covered in this book.

If you're in Wales, WJEC's GCSE English Language is structured in a different way. Ask your teacher for more information.

The Front Page tells you What To Do

First up — <u>what to do</u> when you plonk yourself down in that nice, comfy exam chair (there's more on the <u>structure</u> of the <u>Unit 1 exam</u> on the next page):

1) The <u>front page</u> of the question paper will tell you what you should have in front of you. Read it through and make sure you've <u>got everything</u>. Here's what you should have for the <u>Unit 1 exam</u>:

   • A <u>question paper</u> which will have all the <u>questions</u> and <u>one</u> of the <u>non-fiction texts</u> you'll be asked about.

   • A <u>separate booklet</u> (called the Resource Material) containing the other <u>non-fiction text</u>.

   • A <u>12-page answer book</u> to write your answers in.

2) Make sure you fill in all the <u>details</u> you're asked for on the <u>front</u> of the answer book, or you won't get any marks at all — not ideal.

3) Make sure you've got the <u>higher tier</u> paper, not the foundation one.

4) Read all the <u>instructions</u> on the front page of the question paper to remind you what to do.

My mum tells me what to do...

So there you are, just two exams for your GCSE in English or English Language. There are controlled assessments to do for Unit 3 and Unit 4 as well, but they're for another day — all we're looking at in this book is Unit 1. It's the most fun bit anyway, at least, that's what I think.

Summary of the Exam

This page is about the different <u>questions</u> on the Unit 1 exam, and how many <u>marks</u> each one's wort
Crikey, with all this info to take in about the exam, they'll be giving you an exam on the exam next...

The <u>Unit 1 exam is worth</u> 40 Marks

1) The whole exam is worth <u>40 marks</u>, and counts for <u>30%</u> of your total GCSE mark
   (for either GCSE English Language or GCSE English).

2) The questions are most often worth <u>10 marks each</u>, so the exam usually has <u>four</u>
   <u>10 mark questions</u>.

3) Sometimes though, some of the questions will be worth <u>5 marks</u>. So, for example, the
   exam might have <u>five questions</u> — <u>two</u> worth 5 marks and <u>three</u> worth 10 marks. Sneaky.

The <u>Unit 1 exam is based on</u> Two Pieces <u>of</u> Non-Fiction Text

1) The Unit 1 exam will be based on <u>2 pieces of non-fiction text</u> that
   you haven't seen before — one will be in the <u>question paper</u> and the
   other will be in the <u>separate booklet</u> you're given in the exam.

2) The texts you'll be given could be anything from <u>leaflets</u>, <u>letters</u>,
   <u>reports</u>, <u>biographies</u>, <u>articles</u> (from <u>newspapers</u>, <u>magazines</u>,
   <u>brochures</u> or the <u>internet</u>), <u>advertisements</u> or <u>fact sheets</u>.

In his exam, James was faced with a type of text he had never seen before.

3) For one of the questions you'll have to <u>compare</u> the two texts —
   this will usually be the <u>last question</u>.

4) All the other questions will each be on <u>one</u> of the two texts. For example, if there are four
   questions the first two could be on the <u>first text</u>, the third question could be on the <u>other text</u>
   and the final question could be on <u>both</u>.

5) Make sure you read the questions properly (you'll be told which text you should write about)
   so that your answer is about the <u>right text or texts</u>.

Answer All the Questions

1) You have to answer <u>every question</u> in the Unit 1 exam.

2) You have <u>one hour</u> for this exam — that <u>includes</u> the time you'll spend <u>reading</u> the texts
   you've been given.

> You should spend a total of about <u>7-8 minutes reading</u>
> <u>each text</u> and about <u>45 minutes writing your answers</u>.

3) If there are <u>four 10 mark questions</u>, you should spend about <u>11 minutes</u> answering each one.

4) If there are any <u>5 mark questions</u> in the exam, you should spend about <u>5-6 minutes</u> answering
   them (and still about <u>11 minutes</u> on the <u>10 mark questions</u>).

That's the theory sorted — turn over to see an exam...

Now you know how the exam is structured, I bet you're dying to have a look at an actual paper.
Well, I was feeling nice today so I made one just for you — take a look at the next few pages.

Exam Paper — Questions

Here are some lovely <u>example questions</u> — similar to the ones you'll get in your Unit 1 exam.
The texts are printed on the next two pages.

*The **Resource Material** is a magazine article entitled 'The Spice is Right!'*
written by Emily Goodwin.

The other item is a newspaper article entitled 'Vindaloo? No thank you.'
by Linda Marchant.

**Look at the magazine article by Emily Goodwin
('The Spice is Right!') on the following page.**

Make sure you include plenty of examples from the article in your answer.

1.   According to this article, why is eating Indian food good for you?

[10 marks]

2.   How does Emily Goodwin try to make her article interesting for her readers?

Think about:
*   what she says;
*   how she says it;
*   the use of headlines and subheadings;
*   the use of pictures and captions.

Remember to write about each of the bullet points.

[10 marks]

**Now look at the newspaper article by Linda Marchant
('Vindaloo? No thank you').**

Describe the writer's opinions in your own words, and use short quotes to back up your points.

3.   What are Linda Marchant's opinions of the Indian restaurant she visited?

[10 marks]

To answer the next question you will need to look at both texts.

4.   Compare and contrast what Emily Goodwin and Linda Marchant
say about Indian food.

This means you need to write about the similarities and differences between the two texts.

[10 marks]

"How did you find the exam?" "It was just on the table..."

It's important to look at sample exam questions like this to get an idea of what the real exam is like.
You'll notice that certain types of question come up again and again: what are the writer's opinions,
compare and contrast this with that, how does the writer do this, what should I have for tea...

Exam Text: Magazine Article

Here's one of your texts for the exam questions on the previous page.

The Spice is Right!

Have you ever had a craving for curry? When you crave a food, that's your body screaming at you that it needs something. With the huge number of essential nutrients contained in curry, no wonder it's become popular all over the world and is the UK's favourite dish.

Super spices
The ingredients that make curry so tasty are, of course, spices. As well as being able to dazzle your taste buds, many of the most popular spices in curry also have some pretty remarkable health benefits.

© iStockphoto.com/catetus

Rainbow colours: just some of the spices that go into curries

Turmeric is one of the most common spices used in curry. It contains curcumin, which has been shown to kill cancer cells, clear the brain of protein deposits that can cause Alzheimer's disease and decrease joint swelling. Pretty impressive, eh?

But the health benefits don't end there. Many curries also contain chillies, which are rich in Vitamin C (to boost your immune system and help fight colds and flu), Vitamin B6 (to relieve stress), and capsaicin (to increase metabolism and help with weight loss).

> " *curry might hold the key to your peace of mind* "

Other spices, like allspice, star anise, cardamom and black pepper have been used for centuries by Chinese herbalists to relieve digestive problems, clear headaches and help clear the body of toxins.

And if you're prone to anxiety or insomnia, or are trying to give up smoking, then curry might hold the key to your peace of mind. Cloves have been shown to decrease nicotine cravings, whilst coriander is a natural relaxant, and its sedative properties have been recognised in Iran for generations.

The tasty way to your 5 a day!
If you're not already dashing to your local Indian restaurant for a plate of their finest jalfrezi, then perhaps the thought of not having to plough through a tonne of salad to get your 5 a day might convince you.

We wouldn't recommend eating chillies for all five of your portions.

By choosing a vegetable curry, or adding a few carrots or green beans to your lean meat, it's easy to get a healthy, low-fat curry that's high in fibre and packed full of nutritious vegetables.

Some like it hot, others... don't
It doesn't even matter if you don't like your food too hot and spicy, there's so much variety in Indian food that there's bound to be a dish that'll suit you down to the ground. For example, milder curries like korma or pasanda are made with cream and subtle spices that won't leave you with third-degree burns in your mouth. Of course, for the daredevils amongst you, there are much more dangerous options: madras and vindaloo will test your taste buds to breaking point.

Get the hots for curry
Eating Indian food isn't just about the health benefits or the delicious taste though, it can be a great social occasion. Whether you're with family, friends or both you can add to the buzz by sharing one or two of your favourite dishes. So make sure you don't just have curry as a special treat or a Friday night craving-fix; it should be a regular addition to mealtimes. It's easy to make — check out our recipe pages for ideas — or if you're feeling adventurous you could experiment and create your own. So stock up on your turmeric and coriander, and get cooking!

Emily Goodwin

Exam Text: Newspaper Article

Here's the other text for those fun-looking exam questions on page 41.

Vindaloo? No thank you.

Linda Marchant
Sunday June 20th 2010
The Chronicle

The English take on Indian food curries no favour with Linda Marchant.

It's Friday night, and I've arranged to meet an old university friend for dinner at a new Indian restaurant in town.

First impressions are uninspiring: the exterior looks more like an office than an Indian restaurant. Inside, the decor is dominated by glass and chrome, with an entire wall devoted to a giant fish tank. The speakers blast out Shakira, and Bombay seems a million miles away.

I consider leaving, but it's too late — I've been spotted by the severely bored-looking waiter, who leads me to our table.

Ah well, I'm here now, I might as well make the best of it, and I do love a good curry. When it's done properly, authentic Indian food can be a truly mind-blowing experience with an incredible variety of flavours, so perhaps I won't be disappointed after all. I glance through the pages of my menu, which features a mishmash of dishes — tandoori, pasanda, makhani and (shudder) tikka masala, that authentic Indian curry, invented in Glasgow in the 1970s. I favour something a bit spicier, so perhaps the specials board will satisfy my needs. Some hope. It would seem that I've accidentally stepped into a bizarre Anglo-Indian-Italian hybrid country, where steak and chips nestle happily next to gnocchi. My mistake, I must have misread the sign that said 'Authentic Indian Cuisine'.

Would you eat something this colour? Takeaway chicken tikka masala, calories: 684, fat: 27g.

It's a busy evening, and after a longish wait, our waiter arrives to take our order. Another great thing about Indian food is how different dishes complement each other, so I ask for a mango lassi (a kind of yoghurt drink) to counteract the spiciness of the curry. However, since all I get in return is a blank look, I decide the easiest thing to do is order a coke. As for the food, I love a good jalfrezi, as long as it's made with fresh chilli, so I decide to quiz our waiter about the types of spices used.

"We use curry powder," he explains slowly and clearly, as if I might be an escapee from the local asylum. So what's the difference between the jalfrezi and, say, the rogan josh then?

"The jalfrezi's a hot curry, so we put *more* curry powder in it, madam." He smiles encouragingly, pleased at having enlightened the poor stupid customer. I sigh and decide to risk a vegetable jalfrezi — it may not be great, but they can't go too far wrong with vegetables, tomatoes and curry powder, right? Wrong.

The food arrives, a dish of fluorescent orange slop with a side dish of olives (yes, olives) and over-cooked rice. It's over-salted, under-spiced and, weirdly, tastes *exactly* the same as my friend's chicken dhansak.

It's a real shame, as Indian food can be delicious. The right combination of spices, carefully selected meat and vegetables and light, fluffy rice can provide a tantalising (yet healthy) curry. All too often, as is the case here, the curries are stuffed full of salt, saturated fat and excess calories, as well as completely unnecessary additives and colourings. Innocent diners, naively believing a curry with vegetables in to be a healthy option, are unaware of the fact that it probably contains their fat and calorie allowance for the whole month.

Sadly, this restaurant seems to have given up on those customers who want a decent curry. They favour the drunken, Saturday night, post-nightclub rabble, who wouldn't know a chilli from a chapati, and don't care if their meal glows in the dark.

Until these restaurants get their act together and start serving curry as it's meant to be — jam-packed with contrasting flavours, fresh veg and aromatic spices — I think I'll stick to making my own.

Mark Scheme

These pages show you just how an examiner would mark the exam questions on page 41, so that you know exactly what to do to please them. Ooh, isn't it subversive...

How they work out your Grade

Mark the four questions individually using the mark schemes on pages 44-47.
Then <u>add up</u> the four marks and use the table below to get your mock Unit 1 <u>grade</u>.

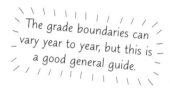
The grade boundaries can vary year to year, but this is a good general guide.

Marks	20-23	24-27	28-31	32-35	36-40
Grade	D	C	B	A	A*

Of course, your final GCSE English or English Language grade is an <u>average</u> of this, your <u>Unit 2</u> exam and your <u>controlled assessments</u>. But the grade you get for this exam shows the grade you're <u>on course for</u>.

If you're taking your exams in Wales, this GCSE has a different structure. Check the mark information with your teacher.

Question 1

1. According to this article, why is eating Indian food good for you?   [10 marks]

Here are some possible Points for an Answer

Here are some <u>points</u> that could be given in an answer. Other <u>valid points</u> would also gain marks.

- Eating Indian food is good for you because curries contain a "huge number of essential nutrients" that your body "needs".
- Turmeric, which is often used in curries, contains an ingredient which can "kill cancer cells", as well as help to prevent Alzheimer's disease and "decrease joint swelling".
- Curry can be good for people who are "prone to anxiety or insomnia". This is because it often contains coriander, which is a "natural relaxant".

Here's a Marking Grid for question 1

Mark	Quality of Answer
0 marks	Nothing written that helps to answer the question.
1 mark	Simple comments with a few references to the text, or just copying large chunks of it. Most comments don't really answer the question, and may misinterpret the text.
2-4 marks	Simple comments about the basic ideas of the text, showing understanding of the obvious reasons why Indian food is good for you. Some relevant examples from the text are given.
5-7 marks	Makes several valid points which clearly show why Indian food is good for you, backed up with relevant examples from the text. There are few, if any, irrelevant points made.
8-10 marks	Selects and explains a wide range of valid points, to show a clear understanding of both the text and the question. Answer is written fluently and in full, well-structured sentences.

Mark Scheme

Question 2

> 2. How does Emily Goodwin try to make her article interesting for her readers?
> Think about:
> - what she says;
> - how she says it;
> - the use of headlines and subheadings;
> - the use of pictures and captions. [10 marks]

Here are some possible Points for an Answer

This question tests your ability to explain how the writer has used different techniques to engage the reader. Here are some points you could think about, but again, these are just suggestions.

What she says:
- Emily Goodwin says that curry is "the UK's favourite dish" and is "popular all over the world". This emphasises how popular Indian food is, so the reader would be interested to find out why.

How she says it:
- She addresses the reader directly, "stock up on your turmeric and coriander, and get cooking!". This creates an informal tone, which makes the article interesting to the reader because it feels like they are being offered advice by a friend, rather than by someone they don't know.

The use of headlines and subheadings:
- The headline makes the reader interested in the article. It says "The Spice is Right!" which shows that it is about spices and how they are a good thing. However, it doesn't say anything else, so the reader would need to read the article to find out what is "Right" about the spices.

The use of pictures and captions:
- There's a bright and eye-catching photograph of the different spices and herbs used to make Indian food. They look exotic and tantalising and some readers wouldn't know much about them, so they would want to read the article to find out more.

Here's a Marking Grid for question 2

Mark	Quality of Answer
O marks	Nothing written that helps to answer the question.
1 mark	Simple comments on the article, or just copying large chunks of the text.
2-4 marks	Simple comments that show a basic understanding of the obvious features that make the article interesting. Some examples used and some attempt made to explain how they make the article interesting.
5-7 marks	Makes several valid points which clearly show how the features of the article make it interesting, using relevant examples from the text. All four bullet points are covered.
8-10 marks	Selects a wide range of techniques used and explains in detail how they are used to interest the reader. Answer is written fluently and in clear, well-structured sentences.

Mark Scheme

Question 3

3. What are Linda Marchant's opinions of the Indian restaurant she visited?

[10 marks]

Here are some possible Points for an Answer

This question tests your ability to pick out the writer's <u>thoughts</u> from the article. Here are some points you could make — but remember, there may be <u>other valid points</u> too.

- The writer is unimpressed with the appearance of the restaurant. She describes it as "uninspiring" and thinks it "looks more like an office than an Indian restaurant". It obviously doesn't match her idea of what an Indian restaurant should look like, because she says "Bombay seems a million miles away".
- Linda Marchant doesn't think the restaurant serves "authentic" Indian food. She sees that the menu has "(shudder) tikka masala, that authentic Indian curry, invented in Glasgow in the 1970s" on it. By using the word "shudder" she is imitating the action people make when they really dislike something, which shows that she's being sarcastic when she says it is an "authentic Indian curry".
- Linda Marchant thinks the service in the restaurant is poor. She receives a "blank look" from the waiter when she tries to order a traditional Indian drink, which shows that she thinks either the waiter is ignorant, or that the restaurant doesn't serve something it should.
- She is disgusted by the food the restaurant serves when she tries it. She describes her food as "a dish of fluorescent orange slop". The word "fluorescent" makes it sound like the food is radioactive and potentially dangerous to eat.

Here's a Marking Grid for question 3

Mark	Quality of Answer
0 marks	Nothing written that helps to answer the question.
1 mark	Simple comments with a few references to the article, or just copying large chunks of it. Most comments don't really answer the question, and may misinterpret the text.
2-4 marks	Simple comments showing a basic understanding of Linda Marchant's more obvious opinions about the restaurant she visited. May use some examples from the text.
5-7 marks	Makes several valid points that show Linda Marchant's opinions. Relevant examples are used, and some explanation of how the examples show her opinions is offered.
8-10 marks	Clearly explains a wide range of valid points about Linda Marchant's opinions of the restaurant she visited, and backs up the points with relevant examples. Answers are written fluently and in full, well-structured sentences.

Mark Scheme

Question 4

> **4.** Compare and contrast what Emily Goodwin and Linda Marchant say about Indian food. [10 marks]

Here are some possible Points for an Answer

You're being tested on how well you can make <u>comparisons</u> between the two texts. Here are a few examples of <u>good points</u> you could make:

- Emily Goodwin says that curry is good for you, and lists the numerous "health benefits" of eating Indian food, for example eating curries with vegetables in can be a "tasty way to your 5 a day". In contrast, Linda Marchant says that curries are often "full of salt, saturated fat and excess calories", as well as containing "completely unnecessary additives and colourings". However, she does acknowledge that, when cooked properly, Indian food can be "healthy".

- Both Goodwin and Marchant are clearly in favour of Indian food in general: Goodwin refers to it as "the UK's favourite dish", and says that it can "dazzle your taste buds", while Marchant states "Indian food can be delicious" and a "truly mind-blowing experience". However, Marchant is ultimately disappointed with the "over-salted, under-spiced" food she is served in the restaurant she visits.

- Emily Goodwin describes how eating curry can be a "great social occasion", whereas Linda Marchant criticises the "drunken, Saturday night, post-nightclub rabble" that some Indian restaurants cater for. Goodwin's "buzz" from "sharing one or two of your favourite dishes" contrasts sharply with Marchant's description of drunken diners "who wouldn't know a chilli from a chapati, and don't care if their meal glows in the dark".

Here's a Marking Grid for question 4

Mark	Quality of Answer
0 marks	Nothing written that helps to answer the question.
1 mark	Simple comments with a few references to the texts, or just copying large chunks of them. Most comments don't really answer the question.
2-4 marks	Makes some simple comparisons based on the obvious things the writers say about Indian food. May focus on one text more than the other.
5-7 marks	Makes several valid comparisons between the texts, with examples from both texts used to back up points. The answer covers both texts in about the same amount of detail.
8-10 marks	Makes clear, detailed comparisons between the texts using appropriate cross references. Answer talks about both texts equally and is written fluently in full, well-structured sentences.

Grade C & B Answers to Question 1

These two pages show you <u>example answers</u> for <u>question 1</u>, starting with a <u>"C" grade answer</u> and working all the way up to an <u>"A*"</u>. Look back at pages 41-43 for the exam questions and texts.

Question 1 is about Finding Information

1) The first question is usually the easiest to get a few marks on. It's testing to make sure you've <u>understood</u> the text and can <u>find information</u>.

2) Read the <u>whole article</u> carefully. You could use a highlighter pen to <u>identify</u> the <u>points</u> you're going to use in your answer.

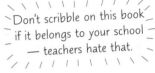
Don't scribble on this book if it belongs to your school — teachers hate that.

Here's a <u>"C" grade</u> answer to question 1.

> The writer says that Indian food is good for you because it contains "essential nutrients". The article also gives lots of examples of how your health can benefit from eating the different spices you get in curry. For example, turmeric "contains curcumin, which has been shown to kill cancer cells". Some of the other spices used in curry can even help you to give up smoking, or get over problems like anxiety and insomnia.
>
> Curries can be packed full of nutritious vegetables, which helps you get your 5 a day. These kinds of curries are "high in fibre" and "low-fat", so they are very good for you. The writer says that curry is "the UK's favourite dish".

This is a good example to back up the point that's being made.

This bit should be in quotation marks as it's taken straight from the article.

This doesn't answer the question.

This answer is a start, but it needs to make <u>more points</u> and use more <u>examples</u> to get a higher mark. Everything in the answer should also be <u>relevant</u> to the question.

Use Examples from the text to Back Up your points

1) This question is just asking you to write about <u>why</u> Indian food is <u>good for you</u> — don't go off writing about <u>anything else</u>.

2) Back up your points with lots of <u>short</u>, <u>snappy quotes</u>.

Here's a <u>"B" grade</u> answer to the question.

> The article describes the "remarkable health benefits" of Indian food, saying that curry contains lots of "essential nutrients" that your body "needs".
>
> It's mostly the spices used in Indian food that are really good for you though. Turmeric "has been shown to kill cancer cells, clear the brain of protein deposits that can cause Alzheimer's disease and decrease joint swelling". Chillies contain lots of vitamins that do things like "boost your immune system", and other spices, such as cardamom, can "relieve digestive problems, clear headaches and help clear the body of toxins".
>
> Goodwin tells us that adding vegetables to a curry is "The tasty way to your 5 a day", so curries can help you to eat more vegetables which are good for you because they are "nutritious". She also says that vegetable curries are "healthy, low-fat" and "high in fibre", so you could eat them and you won't put on too much weight.

Short quotes like this are good.

Don't copy out big chunks of the text — it makes it look like you haven't understood it.

This is good — it doesn't just say that eating vegetables in curries is good for you, it explains <u>why</u>.

This is a good answer because it's made several <u>good points</u> and <u>explained</u> them well.

Grade A & A* Answers to Question 1

You need to show that you've Understood the article

1) You should show you've understood all the key points in the article.

2) Your quotations and evidence should really add to what you're saying, not just prove it.

Here's an "A" grade answer to question 1.

Good opening — gets straight to the point of the question.

> According to Emily Goodwin, Indian food is good for you because it contains a "huge number of essential nutrients". She suggests that a "craving for curry" is actually a craving for the nutrients that your body "needs".
>
> Goodwin backs up this claim by stating the "remarkable health benefits" of the main spices used to make curry. Turmeric can "kill cancer cells", help prevent Alzheimer's disease and "decrease joint swelling", while coriander is a "natural relaxant", so it can help you get to sleep. Chillies, meanwhile, are "rich" in vitamins C and B6 and capsaicin, which have many different health benefits. Spices such as star anise can help "clear headaches" and "relieve digestive problems" while cloves can "decrease nicotine cravings" so they can help you to give up smoking.
>
> Another health benefit of eating curry comes if you add "nutritious vegetables" to your meal. Vegetables make the curry "high in fibre" and "low-fat", and also provide a "tasty way to your 5 a day", which ensures that you have a balanced, healthy diet.

This could do with a bit more explanation.

Make sure your answer is Organised

1) Your answer should clearly and concisely describe what you learn from the article.

2) There are 10 marks available, so try and make ten different points to get top marks.

Here's an "A*" grade answer to the question.

> Emily Goodwin's article highlights many "remarkable health benefits" associated with curry. It is full of "essential nutrients" that your body "needs" to be healthy, which reveals that Indian food is good for you.
>
> The spices used in Indian food can improve your physical health: turmeric contains curcumin, which helps "kill cancer cells" and get rid of "protein deposits" in the brain that can lead to Alzheimer's disease. Curcumin also helps to "decrease joint swelling". The vitamins found in chillies (vitamin C and Vitamin B6) "boost your immune system" and "relieve stress", while chillies also contain capsaicin, which can "help with weight loss". The article also lists a group of spices ("allspice, star anise, cardamom and black pepper") that remove "toxins" from the body, cure headaches and help with digestive problems.
>
> Eating Indian food can improve your mental health as well: the article claims that "curry might hold the key to your peace of mind". This is because spices such as cloves "decrease nicotine cravings" so they can help you "give up smoking", while coriander is a "natural relaxant", so it can help with problems like "anxiety or insomnia".
>
> The article also tells us that having a vegetable curry (or adding vegetables to a meat curry) can provide you with one or more portions of the "5 a day" that are recommended for a healthy lifestyle. The vegetables help to make the curry "low-fat" and "high in fibre", both of which are important in a healthy diet.

This is good — it hasn't missed out any of the details.

This answer is structured well — a new point is in a new paragraph.

The article doesn't say this explicitly — it shows you've really understood it.

Grade C & B Answers to Question 2

So that's question 1 done — now for question 2. Remember, the exam's on pages 41-43.

For question 2, you need to write about Each Bullet Point

1) For each point you make, back it up with an example from the text.

2) Then you need to explain what effect the techniques used have on the reader, and say why they make the article interesting — remember P.E.E.D. (see page 33).

Here's a "C" grade answer to question 2.

\ Examples don't have t ~ be quotations — it's - fine to describe the / pictures used.

\Avoid general statements / like these — you need to explain how the technique makes the article interesting.

> The colourful pictures of some chillies and other spices make the article look interesting. The spices look exciting and the reader might not know what they are, so they'll have to read the article to find out. The headline and subheadings are in bold, which makes them stand out more. She tells you lots of facts about curry and the spices that are used, for example, "Cloves have been shown to decrease nicotine cravings", so readers will learn something from the article. The caption next to the photograph of seven chillies is supposed to be funny. The whole article is written in quite chatty language, which means people won't get bored while they are reading it.

\ This point needs to b ~ explained a bit more - — talk about the effe of the funny caption.

This answer makes a few good points, but it isn't very well organised and some of the points need an example or a bit more explanation.

Think about what makes the article Interesting

1) You need to focus on how the writer makes the article interesting.

2) Try and use short quotes often to back up your points.

Here's a "B" grade answer to the question.

~ This could do with ~ an example.

Good — comments on the effect of the picture.

> The author provides the reader with a lot of information, for example "coriander is a natural relaxant". This makes the article more interesting for the reader because they might learn something new by reading it. She also makes the article more exciting for the reader by using words like "daredevils" and "dangerous". Goodwin uses the pronoun "you" throughout the article to make the reader feel like she is talking directly to them. This also helps to make her language more informal and friendly, so the reader will enjoy reading the article more. The subheadings help to break the text up and inform the reader what each section is about. The photographs of chillies and spices are bright and colourful, which grabs the reader's interest. They look appealing so people might want to know how to use them in their cooking. The caption "Rainbow colours" links to the colours in the pictures and makes the food sound more appealing.

\ The bullet point about headings need to be covered in mor detail — it's a bit brief at the moment

Most of the points made are explained well, but some are still a bit vague. A bit more about the headline and subheadings would improve it as well.

Grade A & A* Answers to Question 2

Keep your answer Organised

1) Keep your answer <u>well structured</u> — write a <u>paragraph</u> to cover each <u>bullet point</u> in the question.

2) Make sure your answer is <u>balanced</u> by writing about the <u>same amount</u> for each bullet point.

Here's an <u>"A" grade</u> answer to question 2.

Good use of quotation.

Emily Goodwin writes about the "health benefits" of eating Indian food. For example chillies, often used in curries, contain Vitamin C which will "boost your immune system". Lots of people care about their health and will want to know how to adjust their diet to improve their health, so they would find this article interesting.

This develops the point well.

Goodwin addresses the reader directly, "test your taste buds". This will interest the reader because it sounds like the article has been written specifically for them. Using the pronoun "you" also gives the article an informal tone, so it feels like a friend is letting you in on a secret about how good curries are for you.

It doesn't say how this makes the article interesting.

The headline, "The Spice is Right!", tells the reader that the article is about spices. It uses positive language ("Right!") and an exclamation mark to emphasise that spices are a good thing, but it doesn't say why they are.

The pictures have been selected to make the article look appealing: they are bright, exotic and interesting. The picture on the left shows a range of colourful spices, and the caption informs us that these are "just some" of the spices available, implying that there are many more for readers to find about.

You need to show you Understand the Techniques used

1) You should include lots of <u>detailed evidence</u> to back up your points.

2) Use <u>technical terms</u> and focus on the <u>effect</u> on the reader.

This is an <u>"A*"</u> grade answer to question 2.

Goodwin uses positive vocabulary throughout the article, describing curry as a "popular" dish that is "tasty" and "delicious". This makes curry sound very appealing and would encourage the reader to find out more about it. Readers would also be interested in the article because it makes curry sound exciting: hotter curries are a "dangerous" option for "daredevils". To reinforce this idea, Goodwin presents the alternative, "having to plough through a tonne of salad", as much less exciting than eating curry.

Really good development of the point.

The writer uses a rhetorical question, "Pretty impressive, eh?", after listing some of the health benefits of curry, which engages the reader's interest by making them respond to the question. It is interesting because it makes the reader think about the health benefits of Indian food, and since most readers would probably answer "yes" to this, it encourages them to agree with what the article says.

Confident use of technical terms.

The title, "The Spice is Right!" attracts the reader's interest by using positive language: saying spices are "Right" makes the reader want to read on to find out why. Also, setting the title at an angle, and putting it in a bright yellow spiky box gives the impression that the article will be quirky and fun, which would be interesting to the reader.

The pictures used are bright and eye-catching and the spices and herbs look healthy, fresh and tasty so people would want to know more about them. The caption with the picture of the chillies is also humorous. Even though it sounds like serious advice, most people know that chillies are very hot so it would be unpleasant to eat lots of them. This helps the reader to be entertained by the article.

Good — thinking about the effect of the humour.

Grade C & B Answers to Question 3

Here are some sample answers for question 3.

Focus on the writer's Opinions

1) This question is asking you to give the writer's opinions in your own words, using short quotes as evidence.

2) It's a bit different to question 1, as you have to work out what the writer thinks rather than just understanding what she says.

This is a "C" grade answer to question 3.

This quote is too long — it just copies out a big chunk of the text.

This is good — a ni short quotation.

This could do with an example to back it up.

> Linda Marchant doesn't like the look of the restaurant from outside as she says "First impressions are uninspiring: the exterior looks more like an office than an Indian restaurant". She isn't impressed by the menu "which features a mishmash of dishes — tandoori, pasanda, makhani and (shudder) tikka masala". She eventually orders a vegetable jalfrezi, thinking "they can't go too far wrong with vegetables, tomatoes and curry powder." However, when the food arrives she is very disappointed with it as it looks like "fluorescent orange slop". She says that her food is "over-salted" and "under-spiced" so it is clear that she thinks the food in the restaurant is terrible. She also thinks the waiter is annoying and he isn't very helpful.

This answer makes some good points, but generally doesn't use examples from the text very well.

Organise your answer so it's Easy to Follow

1) It's a good idea to jot down the writer's opinions of the restaurant in a quick plan so you can organise them into separate points.

2) You need to make sure you explain how your examples show the writer's opinions.

Here's a "B" grade answer to the question.

Good opening sentence — gets straight to the point.

This is a good explanation of how the quote shows the writer's opinion.

This is a well-developed point.

> The article's title, "Vindaloo? No thank you", immediately tells us that Linda Marchant didn't like the restaurant. It sounds like if she was offered another meal there she would turn it down. The first paragraph emphasises this by using a pun. She says that the English version of Indian food she received in the restaurant "curries no favour" with her.
>
> Her first impression of the restaurant is that it is "uninspiring". She doesn't think that the atmosphere is very authentically Indian, saying "Bombay seems a million miles away". She finds the restaurant "bizarre" as it doesn't just make Indian food, even though the sign said "Authentic Indian Cuisine". She's also disappointed to find tikka masala on the menu, as it was "invented in Glasgow", not in India.
>
> It is clear that she doesn't think the food will be very good as she decides to "risk" a jalfrezi, which suggests that she doesn't trust anything on the menu. When the food arrives, she is unimpressed as it is "over-salted, under-spiced and, weirdly, tastes exactly the same as my friend's chicken dhansak." It's obvious she won't be eating there again.

This answer is quite good as it backs up each point with an appropriate quotation. Some of the points need to be explained more clearly though.

Grade A & A* Answers to Question 3

Try and Interpret what the article says

1) Go through the article from <u>start</u> to <u>finish</u>, mentioning each of the writer's opinions <u>in turn</u>.

2) You need to show that you understand <u>what the writer means</u>.

Here's an "A" grade answer to question 3.

> Linda Marchant first writes about the appearance of the restaurant. She says that it looks "more like an office than an Indian restaurant", which shows that she thinks it hardly looks like a restaurant at all, let alone an authentic Indian one. She also comments on the decorations inside and the music being played. Her comment that "Bombay seems a million miles away" emphasises her view that the restaurant isn't very authentically Indian.
>
> Marchant's disgust at the lack of authenticity is confirmed by the menu, which is "a mishmash" of dishes from India, England and Italy. She says "I must have misread the sign that said 'Authentic Indian Cuisine'". She is being sarcastic when she says that she misread the sign: it is obvious that she didn't misread it, and she thinks that the restaurant is advertising itself as something that it is not.
>
> When her food arrives she describes it as a plate of "fluorescent orange slop" that is "over-salted" and "under-spiced". The negative implications of the words she uses show that she thinks the food the restaurant serves both looks, and tastes, disgusting.

This is a good way to link the second paragraph to the first.

Explains how what she's written shows what she thinks.

Show that you really Understand the Writer's Opinions

1) Think about what's <u>implied</u> by the article — the writer might <u>not</u> say what she thinks <u>directly</u>.

2) Keep your answer <u>organised</u> — <u>separate</u> her opinions on different things into <u>different paragraphs</u>.

This is an "A*" grade answer.

> Linda Marchant does not like the restaurant at all. Her main problem is that she thinks the restaurant is not authentically Indian, despite advertising that it sells "Authentic Indian Cuisine".
>
> She begins by criticising the appearance of the restaurant, saying that it "looks more like an office than an Indian restaurant". She then goes on to describe the menu as a "bizarre Anglo-Indian-Italian hybrid". By using the word "bizarre" she makes it clear that she thinks this is a bad thing. She then takes particular exception to the presence of "(shudder) tikka masala" on the menu. When she says "shudder", she is showing the reader that she is literally shaking with disgust. Because of this, it is obvious she is being sarcastic when she says that tikka masala is an "authentic Indian curry".
>
> Marchant is critical of the service in the restaurant, as the "severely bored-looking" waiter cannot answer her questions properly. Once again, she uses sarcasm to highlight her annoyance; he "smiles encouragingly, pleased at having enlightened the poor stupid customer", even though he hasn't answered her question at all. Her disappointment in his lack of knowledge is clear from her "sigh".
>
> She is disgusted by the "fluorescent orange slop" that she is served, saying it is "over-salted" and "under-spiced". The two sets of hyphenated words really emphasise her disgust. She is further dismayed to find that her meal "tastes exactly the same" as her friend's meal, despite being a completely different dish; she says this is "a real shame" which reveals that she feels let down by the restaurant.

Sums up the article at the beginning — this shows you have overview.

Makes detailed inferences about the text.

Good — works out what the writer is implying.

Grade C & B Answers to Question 4

Last question now. Remind yourself of the questions and texts by looking back at pages 41-43.

Write the Same Amount about Each Text

1) Read the question a couple of times to make sure you really understand what to do — you only need to cover what the texts say about Indian food.

2) Make comparisons between the two texts — find things they say about Indian food that are similar, and things they say that are different.

Here's a "C" grade answer to question 4.

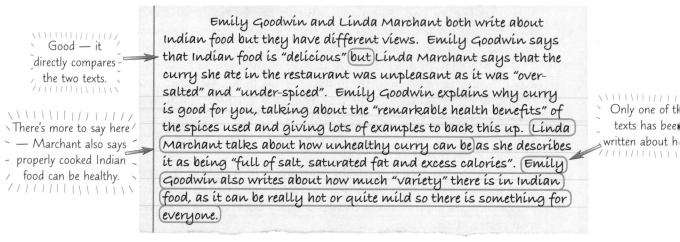

Good — it directly compares the two texts.

There's more to say here — Marchant also says properly cooked Indian food can be healthy.

Emily Goodwin and Linda Marchant both write about Indian food but they have different views. Emily Goodwin says that Indian food is "delicious" but Linda Marchant says that the curry she ate in the restaurant was unpleasant as it was "over-salted" and "under-spiced". Emily Goodwin explains why curry is good for you, talking about the "remarkable health benefits" of the spices used and giving lots of examples to back this up. Linda Marchant talks about how unhealthy curry can be as she describes it as being "full of salt, saturated fat and excess calories". Emily Goodwin also writes about how much "variety" there is in Indian food, as it can be really hot or quite mild so there is something for everyone.

Only one of th[e] texts has been written about h[ere].

This answer makes a couple of good points, but it needs to make more comparisons to get top mark[s].

Use Quotes to Back Up your points

1) Keep your answer organised — make a point about one text, then compare it to the other text.

2) Try and use your own words instead of just copying bits of the text — this shows you've thought about what you're writing.

This is a "B" grade answer to the question.

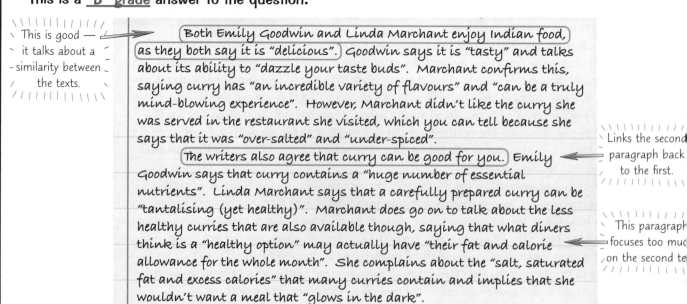

This is good — it talks about a similarity between the texts.

Both Emily Goodwin and Linda Marchant enjoy Indian food, as they both say it is "delicious". Goodwin says it is "tasty" and talks about its ability to "dazzle your taste buds". Marchant confirms this, saying curry has "an incredible variety of flavours" and "can be a truly mind-blowing experience". However, Marchant didn't like the curry she was served in the restaurant she visited, which you can tell because she says that it was "over-salted" and "under-spiced".
The writers also agree that curry can be good for you. Emily Goodwin says that curry contains a "huge number of essential nutrients". Linda Marchant says that a carefully prepared curry can be "tantalising (yet healthy)". Marchant does go on to talk about the less healthy curries that are also available though, saying that what diners think is a "healthy option" may actually have "their fat and calorie allowance for the whole month". She complains about the "salt, saturated fat and excess calories" that many curries contain and implies that she wouldn't want a meal that "glows in the dark".

Links the second paragraph back to the first.

This paragraph focuses too muc[h] on the second te[xt].

This is a pretty good answer, but the second paragraph isn't balanced — it doesn't say enough about the first text.

Grade A & A* Answers to Question 4

Plan your answer to make it Well-Structured

1) Write two quick lists of the things each writer says about Indian food.

2) Put the lists side-by-side so you can compare them and hey presto, you have a plan for your answer.

Here's an "A" grade answer to question 4.

> It is obvious from the articles that both writers love Indian food, but they do also say some different things. While Linda Marchant is of the opinion that "authentic Indian food can be a truly mind-blowing experience", she is let down by the "over-salted, under-spiced" food she is served in an "uninspiring" Indian restaurant. Emily Goodwin, however, says that curry can "dazzle your taste buds" with its "super spices" and "delicious taste". Her article presents a totally positive view of Indian food, but Marchant is let down by restaurants that have "given up" on those who want a "decent curry". Similarly, both writers share the opinion that Indian food can be good for you, but again Marchant highlights that in reality, curries are "All too often" bad for you. Although she says that curries can be "tantalising (yet healthy)", she points out that they are often "stuffed full of salt, saturated fat and excess calories", and are also high in "completely unnecessary additives and colourings". Goodwin, on the other hand, raves about the "remarkable health benefits" of curries, including the spices that "kill cancer cells" and "boost your immune system". She says that curry contains a "huge number of essential nutrients" and that it is easy to have a "healthy, low-fat curry".

This is good — it talks about a similarity and a difference in one go.

Well-chosen examples to back up the point.

Write in a Confident, Fluent way

1) You can show overview (your general impression) by writing a short introduction or conclusion.

2) Relate all your points to Indian food — don't go off writing about anything else.

This is an "A*" grade answer to the question.

This is a really good introduction.

The question's about what the writer's say, so use lots of quotes.

This is a good word to use when you're comparing.

> Both articles discuss curry's potential to be "delicious" and "healthy". However, Emily Goodwin is entirely positive about Indian food, whereas Linda Marchant is disappointed by her experience at a particular Indian restaurant. Goodwin and Marchant are in agreement that Indian food is "delicious", with Goodwin claiming it can "dazzle your taste buds" and Marchant stating that it "can be a truly mind-blowing experience". Marchant's experience in a restaurant though, shows how bad she also thinks Indian food can be. She was served a plate of "fluorescent orange slop" that was "over-salted" and "under-spiced".
> Goodwin makes the point that there is "so much variety" in Indian food, from "milder curries like korma and pasanda" to "more dangerous options: madras and vindaloo". Marchant mentions that a "great thing" about Indian food is the fact that the variety of "different dishes complement each other". However, Marchant's experience showed that there was little variety available in the restaurant she visited. Her vegetable jalfrezi tasted "exactly the same" as her friend's chicken dhansak.
> Goodwin says that curry has "remarkable health benefits" and Marchant agrees that curry can be a "tantalising (yet healthy)" option. Goodwin informs us that curry contains a "huge number of essential nutrients", and the spices used have properties ranging from the ability to "kill cancer cells" to helping you to "give up smoking". However, Marchant does highlight the "salt, saturated fat and excess calories" that many curries contain, and points out that they can be full of "completely unnecessary additives and colourings".

Glossary

alliteration	Where the same sound is repeated at the beginning of words in a phrase. It's often used to make a phrase stand out. E.g. "the <u>b</u>old, <u>b</u>rash <u>b</u>eat of the <u>b</u>and".
analogy	A <u>comparison</u> to show how two things are <u>similar</u>. E.g. "The writer draws an analogy between watching cricket and watching paint dry."
assonance	When words share the same vowel sound, but the consonants are different. E.g. "L<u>i</u>sa had a p<u>ie</u>ce of ch<u>ee</u>se before sh<u>e</u> went to sl<u>ee</u>p, to help her dr<u>ea</u>m."
audience	The people who an author wants to <u>read</u> their writing.
bias	Giving <u>more support</u> to one point of view than to another, due to the writer's <u>own opinions</u> affecting the way they write.
broadsheet	A newspaper like the Daily Telegraph or the Guardian. They're often considered to be more <u>serious</u> and <u>respectable</u> than tabloid newspapers.
caption	A line of text under a photograph or picture, telling you <u>what it shows</u>.
colloquialism	An <u>informal</u> word or phrase that sounds like something said in a <u>conversation</u>. E.g. "Don't keep wittering on about it."
consonants	All the letters in the alphabet that <u>aren't vowels</u>.
context	The <u>background</u> to something, or the situation <u>surrounding</u> it, which affects the way it is written and understood. E.g. "The article was written in the context of the war that was going on."
contrast	When two things are described in a way which emphasises <u>how different</u> they are. E.g. a writer might contrast two different places, or two different attitudes.
counter-argument	A way of arguing a point by first giving the opposite point of view, then <u>disagreeing</u> with it.
emotive language	Language that has an <u>emotional</u> effect on the reader, e.g. making them feel angry
empathy	When someone feels like they <u>understand</u> what someone else is experiencing and how they <u>feel</u> about it.
exaggeration	Describing something as more <u>extreme</u> than it really is. E.g. "A million miles away".
first person	A personal style of writing, using words like "I", "me", "mine", "we", "us", "our" etc
font	The style of <u>type</u> used.
formatting	The way text is laid out on a page, including its font, margins, use of columns, etc.
generalisation	A statement that gives an <u>overall impression</u>, sometimes a misleading one, without going into details. E.g. "Children today eat too much junk food."

Glossary

headline — The statement at the <u>top</u> of a text (e.g. a newspaper article), usually in a <u>large font</u>, used to attract a reader's interest by giving an impression of what it's about.

imagery — Language that creates a <u>picture in your mind</u>, bringing the text to life.

implication — When a writer gives an <u>impression</u> that something is the case <u>without</u> saying it outright. E.g. "Last time I left Steve in charge, the house nearly burnt down" — this <u>implies</u> that Steve can't be trusted, without saying it directly.

inconsistency — When one bit of a text <u>contradicts</u> (disagrees with) another bit, so that the argument doesn't really add up. It's a sign of weakness in an argument.

irony — Saying one thing but <u>meaning the opposite</u>. E.g. "What a great idea of mine to go for a nice long walk on the rainiest day of the year."

language — The <u>choice of words</u> used. The language determines the effect the piece of writing will have on the reader, e.g. it can be emotive or persuasive.

layout — The way a piece of writing is visually <u>presented</u> to the reader. E.g. what kind of <u>font</u> is used, whether there are subheadings, the use of photographs, whether text columns are used, and anything else that affects the way a text looks.

media — Any way of <u>communicating</u> with <u>large numbers</u> of people, e.g. newspapers, TV, radio, films, websites, magazines.

metaphor — A way of describing something by saying that it <u>is something else</u>, to create a vivid image. E.g. "His eyes were deep, black, oily pools."

narrative — A part of a text that tells a <u>story</u> or describes an <u>experience</u>.

non-fiction — Writing about the <u>real world</u>, rather than making up a story.

onomatopoeia — Using words that <u>sound like</u> their meaning. E.g. "buzz", "crunch", "bang", "pop", "ding".

personification — A special kind of description where you write about something as if it's a <u>person</u> or animal with thoughts or feelings. E.g. "The sea growled hungrily."

pun — A "play on words" — a word or phrase that's used humorously because it has <u>more than one meaning</u>. E.g. "She lies on the couch at the psychiatrist's", where "lies" could mean "lies down" or "tells lies".

purpose — The <u>reason</u> someone writes a text. E.g. to persuade, to argue, to advise.

rhetoric — <u>Language</u> techniques that are designed to achieve a specific <u>effect</u>, e.g. repetition or exaggeration to make a speech more persuasive.

rhetorical question — A question which <u>doesn't need an answer</u>. E.g. "Are we really expected to put up with this government's lies?"

Glossary

sarcasm	Saying something in a cutting, <u>nasty</u> way, often using <u>irony</u>. E.g. "Well done Kerry — another failed exam. You really are a bright spark."
satire	A text that <u>makes fun</u> out of someone, or something — e.g. a politician, governmen or organisation. It's often done by imitating someone and exaggerating their flaws.
simile	A way of describing something by <u>comparing</u> it to something else, usually by using the words "like" or "as". E.g. "He was as pale as the moon," or "Her hair was like a bird's nest."
slang	Words or phrases that sound <u>informal</u> or <u>conversational</u>, e.g. "bloke", "telly", "stop going on about it".
stereotype	A <u>generalised</u> view of a particular <u>group of people</u> that is often negative. E.g. a stereotype of football fans might be that they're all hooligans.
structure	The <u>order</u> and <u>arrangement</u> of a piece of writing. E.g. how the text begins, develops ends, and whether it uses subheadings or not.
style	The <u>way</u> a text is <u>written</u>, e.g. the type of language and techniques used.
subheading	A word or phrase that <u>stands out</u> from the text and <u>divides</u> the text into chunks. It gives an idea of what the <u>next section</u> of text is about.
syllable	A single <u>unit of sound</u> within a word. E.g. "all" has one syllable, "always" has two and "establishmentarianism" has nine.
tabloid	A newspaper like the Sun or the Mirror, often thought of as <u>less serious</u> than the broadsheets.
text	Any piece of <u>writing</u>, e.g. an article, a speech, a leaflet.
text formatting	Ways of making bits of text <u>stand out</u>, e.g. **bold**, _italic_, <u>underlining</u>, CAPITALS.
theme	An <u>idea</u> or <u>topic</u> that's important in a piece of writing. E.g. a newspaper article could be based on the theme of third world debt.
tone	The <u>mood</u> of a piece of writing, e.g. happy, sad, serious, lighthearted. It's an overall effect, created by things like choice of words, imagery and layout.
vocabulary	The range of <u>words</u> used by a writer or in a specific text.
voice	The <u>personality</u> of the writer of a text. It can be fairly neutral, as in some broadshe newspaper articles, or very opinionated, like in a tabloid editorial.
vowels	Simple — the letters '<u>a</u>', '<u>e</u>', '<u>i</u>', '<u>o</u>' and '<u>u</u>' (and sometimes '<u>y</u>', e.g. in "happy").

Index

Index